Fossil Ridge Public Library District
386 Kennedy Road
Braidwood, Illinois 60408

11/99

CULTURES OF THE WORLD

CYPRUS

Michael Spilling

MARSHALL CAVENDISH
New York • London • Sydney

Reference edition published 2000 by
Marshall Cavendish Corporation
99 White Plains Road
Tarrytown
New York 10591

© Times Editions Pte Ltd 2000

Originated and designed by
Times Books International, an imprint of
Times Editions Pte Ltd

Printed in Malaysia

Library of Congress Cataloging-in-Publication Data:

Spilling, Michael.
    Cyprus / Michael Spilling.
      p. cm.—(Cultures of the World)
    Includes bibliographical references (p.) and index.
    Summary: Discusses the geography, history, government,
economy, people, and culture of Cyprus, the newest
independent state in the Mediterranean.
    ISBN 0-7614-0978-5 (lib. bdg.)
    1. Cyprus—Juvenile literature. [1. Cyprus.] I. Title.
II. Series.
DS54.A3S65   2000
956.93—dc21   99–31942
                 CIP
                 AC

INTRODUCTION

Strategically located in the eastern Mediterranean, the distinctive, pan-shaped island of Cyprus has, since ancient times, been an attractive base for traders, explorers, colonists, and armies. The mythical birthplace of the Greek goddess Aphrodite, culture upon culture has left its imprint through the ages, with the island playing host to Greeks, Romans, Persians, Arabs, Byzantines, Crusaders, Turks, and British colonists. Today, the country is more often invaded by tourists, a consequence of its dry, warm climate, beautiful beaches, and rapid tourist development.

Despite a complex history, Cyprus is the newest state in the Mediterranean, having gained independence only in 1960. Since 1974, ethnic intolerance and conflict have left the island divided between the dominant ethnic Greek community and the smaller Turkish community. Despite the problems, Cypriots are a relaxed, hospitable people proud of their identity and traditions.

CONTENTS

A Cypriot girl displays the typical warmth and cheerfulness of Cypriots.

4

CONTENTS

The twin minarets of the famous Selimiye mosque are a distinctive feature in Nicosia, the capital of Cyprus.

GEOGRAPHY

THE ISLAND OF CYPRUS lies in the far eastern corner of the Mediterranean Sea, about 40 miles (64 km) south of Turkey, 60 miles (97 km) west of Syria, and 480 miles (772 km) south of mainland Greece. The island is 140 miles (225 km) in length from the northeastern tip of Cape Andreas to the western coast of Cape Arnauti, while only 60 miles (97 km) at its widest point from north to south.

A total area of 3,572 square miles (9,251 square km) makes Cyprus the third largest island in the Mediterranean, after Sardinia and Sicily. Although the island's coastline is generally indented and rocky, most of it is flat and characterized by long, sandy beaches that attract tourists. Visually stunning stretches of coastline occur whenever the hills meet the sea.

Cyprus has four major topographical regions. The Kyrenia Mountains run along the northern coast, while the Troodos Mountains cover a larger area to the south and west. Between the two ranges lies the Mesaoria Plain. To the east and south of the Troodos Mountains are hills.

Politically, Cyprus is divided into the Greek South and the Turkish North, a consequence of longstanding ethnic conflict and the 1974 Turkish invasion. The underpopulated northern area, the Turkish Republic of North Cyprus, makes up about 37% of the island. It includes the Kyrenia Mountains, most of the Mesaoria Plain, the Karpas Peninsula, and the small enclave of Erenköy in the west. The larger, more prosperous Republic of Cyprus in the south consists of the Troodos Mountains and the extensive foothills to the south and west of the mountains.

Above: **A glimpse of the Troodos Mountains, the tallest in Cyprus.**

Opposite: **Wild flowers on the Troodos Mountains. While the geological origins of Cyprus are uncertain, most theories suggest the island was formed by some kind of volcanic explosion.**

7

MOUNTAINS AND PLAINS

Cyprus has two major mountain ranges—the Troodos, formed from molten rock beneath the ocean, and the Kyrenia, part of the Alpine-Himalayan chain that runs through the Eastern Mediterranean.

The Troodos Mountains stretch from the northwest coast for about 50 miles (80 km) to Stavrovouni Peak (2,260 feet / 689 m), which lies about 12 miles (19 km) from the southern coast. At 6,401 feet (1,951 m), Mount Olympus, sometimes known as Mount Troodos, is Cyprus's highest peak. On a clear winter day, a fantastic view can be seen from the northern slopes of Mount Olympus across Morphou Bay to the faraway Toros Mountains in Turkey. In contrast to the Kyrenia Mountains, the foothills and valleys of the Troodos Mountains are undulating and spacious. Two of the most beautiful are the Marathasa and Solea valleys, which cut into the northern slopes of the range. The valleys and folds of the hills conceal a huge number of villages, the highest of which is Prodromos, at 4,600 feet (1,402 m) above sea level.

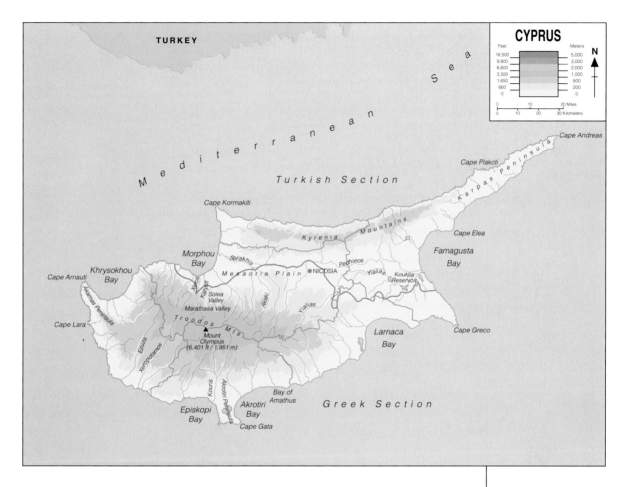

Hugging the northern coast of Cyprus are the narrow, 100-mile (161-km) long Kyrenia Mountains, which are also known as the Pentadaktylos range because one of its most prominent features is a five-fingered peak.

Lying between the two mountain ranges is the flat, low-lying Mesaoria Plain, which stretches from the city of Famagusta on the east coast to Morphou Bay in the west. In the center of the plain lies the capital of Cyprus, Nicosia. Dubbed the breadbasket of Cyprus, the fertile soil of the plain is the principal cereal-growing area of the island, though only half of the land is irrigated. Most of the plain lies in the Turkish part of Cyprus.

The panhandle-shaped area of northeast Cyprus is known as the Karpas Peninsula. The peninsula is remote and undeveloped, an unpolluted, rich source of marine and bird life.

RIVERS AND LAKES

All of the island's major rivers originate in the Troodos Mountains. The largest, the Pedhieos, flows east toward Famagusta Bay. Along with the Yialias, it irrigates much of the Mesaoria Plain. Other major rivers include the Karyoti, which flows north to Morphou Bay, and the Kouris, which flows south toward Episkopi Bay. Much of Cyprus's distinctive appearance comes from the valleys created by these rivers with their deep, gravel beds. All the rivers, which are dry in the summer months, rely on winter rainfall. However, during sudden summer thunderstorms, some of the wadis can turn into raging torrents in less than an hour.

On the south coast, two large saltwater lakes have formed near the towns of Limassol and Larnaca. These lagoons are a rich habitat for bird life, particularly in December and April when birds migrate between Europe and the Nile Delta.

In the summer, the saltwater lake near Larnaca dries, and a crystalline layer forms. Every winter, when the rains come, the lake fills up again.

CLIMATE

Cyprus has an intense Mediterranean climate marked by strong seasonal differences. Summer lasts from June to September, while the winter stretches from November to March. Spring and autumn are short and are characterized by rapid changes in climate and an equally fast transformation of local plant life. Summers are hot and dry, but not humid. The central plain is usually the hottest, with temperatures averaging 99°F (37°C) in Nicosia. Winters are mild, and the weather varies, with average temperatures a cool 41°F–59°F (5°C–15°C). The higher reaches of the Troodos Mountains experience several weeks of below-freezing night temperatures in the winter. Rain generally occurs between October and March, with average annual rainfall of about 20 inches (51 cm). The island's agriculture is dependent on this rainfall, which is often unreliable. The mountain areas receive far more rain than the Mesaoria Plain. Average annual rainfall in Nicosia, for example, is only 14 inches (36 cm), while in the Troodos Mountains, it can be nearly 40 inches (102 cm).

Mount Olympus is covered in snow from January to March.

GEOGRAPHY

Above: **Prickly pear found on the north coast of Cyprus.**

Right: **Pine trees are a well-known feature of the Eastern Mediterranean.**

FLORA

As one of the island's major natural resources, the forests of Cyprus have been extensively exploited for many centuries. This has occurred partly for economic reasons, where the local populace needed wood for export and land for farming. At one time, both the plains and mountains of Cyprus were forested. Today, only 10% of the island is still covered in forest. As early as 400 B.C., the island's rulers placed the local cedar forests under protection, but despite this, the island's forests have continued until modern times to be plundered by both conquerors and locals alike. Today, the remaining forests are high in the Troodos and Kyrenia mountain ranges. Recently, the forestry department has attempted to reverse this trend with extensive replanting.

The predominant tree of the Troodos range is the Aleppo pine, which makes up 90% of all forests in Cyprus. In the upper reaches of the

BLOOMING CYPRUS

Cyprus is one of the richest and most rewarding places to see flowers in the whole of Europe. The island's 1,800 species of flowering plants are characteristic of both Asia Minor and the Mediterranean. These include 170 species of grasses and 90 species of carnation. In April, the height of spring in Cyprus, the island is a blaze of color.

There are 110 species of flowers that can only be found in Cyprus. These include the dark red tulip, *Tulipa Cypria*, and the pinkish-white meadow saffron, *Colchicum Troodi*. The meadow saffron can be found from the Troodos Mountains right down to the coast. Local carnations include *Silene, Petrorhagia, Dianthus,* and *Arenaria*. May is the best month to appreciate the flora of the Troodos Mountains. As soon as the snow melts, flowers such as violets, forget-me-nots, veronica, and crocuses start to bloom. In the lowland areas, wood daisy, Bermuda buttercups, wild cyclamen, and spiny burnet thrive. Orchids are one of the island's most ubiquitous plants. So far, 44 different species or subspecies, as well as numerous hybrids, have been discovered. Examples include the pyramid orchid, the small-leafed helleborine orchid, the buffoon orchid, the Anatolian orchid, and the bee orchid, all of which can also be found in Greece and Turkey. Local varieties include a number of insect orchids, so named because their flowers resemble insects. The rare dotted orchid, with its red and yellow flowers, can also be found. Orchids mainly grow in the Kyrenia Mountains and limestone areas around the Troodos range. All in all, Cyprus is a botanist's delight.

mountains, black pine can also be found. The pine forests are hardy and can resist the extremes of heat and cold. In the Troodos valleys, golden oak and willow can be found. As on many Mediterranean islands, cypress, eucalyptus, and juniper trees are also common. The most famous tree in Cyprus is the cedar. However, today they only grow within the Paphos forest on the slopes of Mount Tripylos, southwest of the island.

Extensive scrub covers the foothills and low-lying areas not under cultivation. The scrub is composed of bulky, thorny bushes of the sclerophyllous variety. The mastic shrub is very common, as are the turpentine tree and the strawberry tree. Rock rose bushes grow over the dry, sun-drenched hills, and can even be found on slopes high in the Kyrenia range. The southern and western slopes of the Troodos are extensively planted with grapevines, while orange groves dominate the area around Morphou Bay. Other cultivated trees include olive, carob, walnut, lemon, grapefruit, fig, date palm, and pomegranate. The Akamas Peninsula is home to more than 500 species of plants, including Aleppo pines, cypress, Phoenician junipers, and carob, oak, and caper trees.

A pelican landing near a waterfront restaurant.

FAUNA

Domestic animals, such as donkeys and oxen, are still a part of village life, and are used for pulling carts and ploughs. Wild donkeys also roam the Karpas Peninsula. However, wild animals are now rare. The only large wild animal now surviving is the agrino, a kind of wild sheep. It is under strict protection in a small forested area of the Troodos range. A type of mouflon, this rare animal has become a symbol of Cyprus, much vaunted in tourist literature. Small game is abundant but aggressively hunted, while foxes, hedgehogs, and shrews can be found all over the island. In contrast to much of the Mediterranean, sheep and goats are rare.

In classical times, snakes were so common that the island was named *Orphiussa*, which means "the abode of snakes." Now snakes are comparatively rare. North of Paphos, the beaches of Cape Lara have become famous for nesting loggerhead turtles, a rare, protected species. The sandy beaches of the Karpas Peninsula also provide similar nesting grounds. Cyprus is home to many lizards because the high temperatures and dry climate provide an ideal environment. The lizards include the impressive starred agama, which grows to a length of 12 inches (30 cm). It lives in rocky crevices and stone walls. The southern slopes of the Kyrenia Mountains are home to the blunt-nosed viper, and climbers occasionally have unwelcome encounters with these ledge-dwelling reptiles. Chameleons also inhabit Cyprus.

Bird life on Cyprus is varied and interesting. Over 300 different species of birds have been documented on the island, the vast majority migratory. The remote and undeveloped Karpas Peninsula is a natural, unpolluted

CONSERVATION OF THE SEA TURTLES

The western coast of the Paphos district is one of the last nesting grounds in the Mediterranean for green and loggerhead turtles, both of which are endangered species. The turtles require dry land to lay their eggs, and so choose deserted, sandy beaches for this purpose. In Cyprus, the turtles nest every two or three years from early June to mid-August. Each turtle lays about 100 eggs every two weeks. The eggs are buried about 20 inches (51 cm) below the sand surface. The hatchlings emerge some seven weeks later and instinctively dash for the sea, which they recognize from reflected moonlight or starlight. Sometimes artificial lights from taverns, hotels, and flashlights distract the newborn turtles, often causing them to move the wrong way and later die of dehydration. Tourist development has narrowed the choice of realistic breeding grounds for turtles, and popular nesting places such as Ayia Napa can no longer be used. Once in the water, the hatchlings are easy prey for seals, sharks, and other large fish. On land, the eggs are sometimes dug up and eaten by foxes. As a result, it is estimated that only one in every 1,000 eggs develops into an adult. Sea turtles only reach maturity 15–30 years after hatching.

Surveys have indicated an alarming drop in the turtle population, and the Cypriot government has set up a project around Cape Lara to try to reverse the decline. The beaches around Cape Lara are off-limits to tourists every summer, when volunteers search the beaches for eggs. If a nest is judged to be poorly sited, the eggs are dug up and moved to a better location with anti-fox wire mesh. The Lara project has yielded good results and has increased the yearly hatchling survival rate fourfold.

habitat for most of the island's birds, and along with the Akamas Peninsula on the west coast, it is one of the few wild places left in Cyprus. More than 160 bird species, 12 mammals, 20 reptiles, and 16 butterfly species have been identified in the Akamas area, including falcons, turtledoves, crested larks, the Cyprus warbler, and Scops's owl. Around the salt lakes of southern Cyprus, flamingos, herons, spoonbills, geese, and ducks can be observed. The salinity of the salt lakes is an ideal habitat for brine shrimp, which make perfect food for flamingos. The Gönyeli reservoir, on the northern edge of Nicosia, is also a good place to see migrating birds.

More northern species such as pigeons, wagtails, blackbirds, finches, and larks visit the island in winter. Rock rose warblers, whitethroats, blue rock thrush, coal tits, wrens, corn bunting, and sparrows are among the birds that nest in Cyprus. The rocky coastal crags of the Kyrenia Mountains are home to griffon vultures, hawks, peregrine falcons, and kestrels. The magnificent griffon vulture has an 8 feet (2.5 m) wingspan.

TOWNS

Cypriots are traditionally a rural people, and the village is the center of their lives. A steady drift of population to the towns began early in the 20th century. This accelerated after the Turkish invasion of the island in 1974 and the consequent need to resettle many refugees in the southern part of the island. Before 1974, only six places were listed as towns—settlements of more than 5,000 people—while 600 villages were recorded. These six towns—Nicosia, Limassol, Larnaca, Paphos, Famagusta, and Kyrenia—constitute the main urban settlements in Cyprus today. They are also the administrative centers for the island's six districts. One result of the Turkish invasion is that the southern, Greek portion of Cyprus is far more populated than the northern, Turkish area. Many of the Cypriots who fled to the south settled around the towns of Limassol, Larnaca, and Paphos, which have grown rapidly since. Nicosia, the capital, remains the only large inland settlement. It is rare for an island capital not to lie on the coast.

NICOSIA, the capital of Cyprus, is a divided city, with the northern portion occupied by Turks and the larger, southern section occupied by Greeks. The capital of Cyprus does not even have a common name—the Turks call it Lefkosa, while the Greeks call it Lefkosia. Nicosia is an old name given to the city by European conquerors. The city has been divided since 1964, when communal violence between Turks and Greeks caused the British to segregate the city. Around 190,000 people live in the Greek portion of the city, while only 40,000 live in the Turkish sector. Nicosia was founded in A.D. 965 by the Byzantine rulers of the island, but only rose to prominence as the administrative capital under Lusignan rule in the 12th–15th centuries. The distinctive, 11-bastioned circular wall of the city center dates from Venetian rule and was built between 1567–1570. The city contains many Greek churches and Muslim mosques, testament to its variable, turbulent history.

In Nicosia, United Nations (UN) peacekeeping forces guard the border crossing, while Greek and Turkish soldiers face each other across the "green line" that cuts the capital in two.

LIMASSOL is a busy trading and tourist center and the island's busiest port. It has a natural harbor, and has been occupied by people since the Bronze Age. Limassol was a Byzantine settlement and later a center for the Crusades. The town did not expand into an important trading center until the late 19th century, when it came under British protection. After the 1974 invasion, the city doubled in size, taking in 45,000 Greek Cypriot refugees. Today, it has a population of 145,000 and is the second largest city on the island. It is estimated that one in three tourists who visit Cyprus spend time on the Bay of Amathus, just east of the town, where a six-mile (10-km) stretch of hotels and man-made beaches joins the town to the 3,000-year-old ruins of Amathus. This, combined with visitors from the nearby British army base, ensures that Limassol has a lively nightlife and cosmopolitan atmosphere.

Around Paphos, a jagged coastline, terraced vineyards, and pine forests combine to form one of the most scenic areas on the island.

LARNACA Farther east along the southern coast is Larnaca, Cyprus's third largest town. Larnaca, which has a population of 64,000, reached its peak in the 19th century, when many international trading offices and consulates were based there for convenience. Since 1974, Larnaca has been the site of the island's international airport. To the east of Larnaca, the land is cramped, a consequence of the Turkish invasion and a demarcation line just to the north of the city. United Nations troops, Greek soldiers, and the many tourists who flock to this city give Larnaca an overcrowded appearance.

PAPHOS Situated on the southwest coast of the island, Paphos is a city with a truly glorious past. In the ancient world, the settlement was a place of pilgrimage throughout the Hellenic world as a center for fertility rituals. Later, the small port became a Roman settlement. Paphos used to be a backward, undeveloped, sparsely populated area. However, this changed in 1982 when an airport was built to develop tourism. Now it has a population of 34,000, and the city is increasingly popular with tourists.

FAMAGUSTA In the Turkish North, there are only two towns of any size, Famagusta and Kyrenia. Founded by Ptolemy II in the third century B.C., Famagusta later fell victim to Arab conquerors, then became a Byzantine conquest in the 12th century A.D. During the Crusades, the town was a thriving center of East-West trade. Following the Ottoman conquest in 1570, the new town of Varosha was established nearby for Christians who had been expelled from Famagusta. Varosha has remained a Greek suburb ever since. Famagusta, like Limassol, has a natural harbor, but since the Turkish invasion in 1974, it is seldom used.

KYRENIA, located on the north coast, was once known as the "Jewel of the Levant" because of its picturesque setting and cosmopolitan social life. Following the 1974 invasion, many Anatolian Turks from the mainland settled here. Today, Kyrenia is a tranquil coastal town of less than 12,000 inhabitants. Most of Kyrenia dates from the medieval and Ottoman periods of rule. It boasts a beautiful harbor, a medieval castle, and a promenade with Venetian-style facades.

Entrance to the old town of Famagusta. *Gazimagusá*, the Turkish name for Famagusta, means "unconquered," a reference to the unsuccessful siege of the town's Turkish quarter by Greek Cypriot forces in 1974.

HISTORY

INVASION AND OUTSIDE DOMINATION have been the norm of 10,000 years of Cyprus's turbulent history. Those who controlled the eastern Mediterranean sought to control Cyprus, an important stepping-stone to the Middle East and Asia Minor. From the earliest times, Cyprus's strategic location has placed the island at the center of numerous epic power struggles between some of the world's great civilizations. Greeks, Persians, Romans, Arabs, and Turks have all left in their wake a residue of splendid monuments and ethnic diversity.

BEGINNINGS

Evidence of human habitation dates from the Neolithic period, before 6000 B.C. Excavations at Khirokitia suggest a settlement of about 2,000 people, living in round, stone houses. The community died out after a few centuries, and the island was uninhabited for the next 2,000 years. The next period of habitation, the Sotira culture, dates from 4500 B.C. The people lived by hunting and fishing. In the copperstone age, dating from 3000 to 2500 B.C., people made tools and pottery from copper.

During the late Bronze Age (1600–1050 B.C.), Cyprus's international contacts extended from the Aegean Sea to the Nile delta and included Syria and Palestine. Mass immigration of Greek-speaking peoples from the Peloponnese occurred in the Iron Age (1100–700 B.C.), establishing the Greek language and six kingdoms on the island—Curium, Paphos, Marion, Soli, Lapithos, and Salamis. Around 800 B.C., a new Phoenician colony was established. Their culture had a great influence on Cyprus.

Above: **Neolithic remains at Khirokitia.**

Opposite: **The Rock of Ramios** *(center, largest rock)* **is believed to be the place where the Greek goddess of beauty and love, Aphrodite, first set foot on the world.**

21

GREEKS AND PERSIANS

In 709 B.C. the kingdoms of Cyprus submitted to Assyrian rule. Its domination ended in 663 B.C., and thereafter, Cyprus enjoyed a century of independence and exuberant, artistic development. Later, Egypt became dominant in the eastern Mediterranean. In 569 B.C. the Cypriot kings were forced to recognize the pharaoh Ahmose II as their ruler.

In 525 B.C. the Cypriot kings shifted their allegiance to the Persian conquerors of Egypt. The Persian expansion embroiled Cyprus in a long battle for dominance between the Greeks and the Persians. When the Ionians revolted against Persian rule in 499 B.C., all the Cypriot kingdoms, except Amathus, joined the revolt. The revolt was suppressed after a year.

Greece and Persia continued to struggle for power in Cyprus. The island became an extremely important naval base in the eastern Mediterranean, and was sought after for its valuable supplies of wood for shipbuilding. King Evagoras I of Salamis succeeded in unifying the island under his rule. However, he was assassinated in 374 B.C.

HELLENESE AND ROMANS

After the swift conquest of the eastern Mediterranean by the Macedonian ruler Alexander the Great, Cyprus willingly integrated into his vast empire (356–323 B.C.). After his death in 323 B.C., the island kingdoms fell into the hands of Ptolemy I of Egypt in 294 B.C., and the island became a Ptolemaic possession for the next 250 years.

In 58 B.C. Cyprus was annexed by the expanding Roman republic. For the next 600 years, Cyprus enjoyed the peace and stability brought about by integration into the Roman and later, Byzantine empires. The island's road network improved, and many public buildings were erected. The Roman garrison remained minimal, and Cypriots went about their affairs with little interference.

A reconstructed Byzantine olive-oil press, used from the seventh to the ninth centuries A.D.

THE BYZANTINE EMPIRE

When the Roman Empire divided in A.D. 395, Cyprus remained a part of the Byzantine Empire. The Arabs, who swept through the eastern Mediterranean in the seventh century, conquered the island in A.D. 649. In A.D. 688 a treaty between Justinian II and the Arab ruler 'Abd al-Malik effectively freed Cyprus from their direct rule for 300 years, introducing an unstable period during which the island was forced to pay tribute to one or the other power, and occasionally both. Cyprus underwent great social changes during this time. There was an influx of Muslims and Arabs, and the island was constantly invaded by Arab forces and harassed by pirates. Many of the cities lay in permanent ruin. However, in A.D. 965 the Byzantine emperor Nicephorus II Phocas regained the island, and a period of economic and cultural prosperity followed.

THE LUSIGNAN KINGDOM

In 1185 the Byzantine governor of Cyprus, Isaac Comnenus, rebelled and declared himself emperor. He was, however, defeated by King Richard I of England during the Third Crusade. Richard later sold the island to Guy of Lusignan, the dispossessed king of Jerusalem.

The Lusignan dynasty (1192–1489) held sway over the island for the next 300 years, although economic competition led to the involvement of Venice and Genoa in Cypriot affairs. During the reign of Peter II (1369–82), both Genoa and Venice competed to control the island's valuable trade. Genoese troops seized Famagusta in 1374, holding it for the next 90 years. The last Lusignan king, Jacques II (reigned 1460–73), regained the throne and managed to expel the Genoese from Famagusta. His wife, Catarina Cornaro, succeeded him, but she ceded Cyprus to Venice during her reign (1474–89). Venice controlled Cyprus for 82 years.

Above: **Richard I is also called Richard the Lionheart, because of his legendary bravery.**

Right: **Ayios Neophytos monastery is famous for its 12th century frescoes.**

OTTOMAN RULE

From their base in the old Byzantine heartland in Turkey, Ottoman power grew in the 16th century, with the capture of Syria, Palestine, and Egypt. In 1570, 350 Turkish ships landed at Larnaca, and the island fell to the Ottomans. Twenty thousand Turks settled on the island after the conquest, while most of the Latin inhabitants emigrated. For the next 300 years, Cyprus became a poor, undeveloped backwater of the Ottoman Empire.

One of the most significant consequences of Ottoman rule was the steady increase in the Turkish population. Turks made up 31% of the island's population by 1841. However, there was little mixing between Turks and Greeks, partly because of their different status under Ottoman rule, but chiefly because of religious differences. A second significant development was the gradual increase in the power of the Orthodox Church. Under the Ottomans, religious leaders were assumed to have political power and responsibilities, resulting in the Orthodox Church becoming increasingly powerful in the Greek community.

Nevertheless, abuses of power and corruption were rife. High taxes were levied in an arbitrary manner on both Greek and Turkish peasants. The rural population grew increasingly dissatisfied with their lot under the thumb of both Turkish rulers and wealthy Orthodox clergy. When the Greek nationalist uprising occurred on the Greek mainland in 1821, a backlash against Greek Cypriots resulted in massacres of local intellectuals and clergymen. Troops were brought in from Syria and Egypt, and a six-month reign of terror left many dead. This caused resentment among the Greeks and an increase in the nationalist feelings the massacres had hoped to quell. Turkish envy rose because of Greek prosperity and higher levels of education. Many poorer rural Turks had become second-class citizens in a country they had conquered only a few hundred years before.

The island suffered a significant fall in population between 1570 and 1740—dropping from 200,000 people in 1570 to 120,000 by 1600, and 95,000 by 1740, following a number of natural disasters and further emigration.

A BRITISH COLONY

The Greek war of liberation marked the beginning of the swift decline of the Ottoman Empire. British power extended to the eastern Mediterranean in the 19th century. Turkey's weakening power and the opening of the Suez Canal in 1869 led the British to exert increasing influence over the Turkish authorities. The Cyprus Convention of 1878 provided that Britain administer the island, which would remain under Turkish sovereignty. The agreement was seen as part of a deal in which the British would reinforce Turkish power against the increasing threat of Russian expansion in the Caucasus. Britain's main concern in supporting Turkey was to ensure that its trade route through the Suez Canal to India remain protected.

With the advent of World War I and a declaration of hostilities between Turkey and Britain in 1914, Britain annexed the island. The island officially became a crown colony in 1925. British rule brought increasing efficiency to the outmoded and corrupt administration of Cyprus. A modern education system was introduced, with separate schools for Christians and Muslims. Cyprus gained from increased contact with Western Europe, and trade boomed for the first time in more than 300 years. A legislative council was formed, consisting of both Cypriots and the British, for making joint administrative decisions. However, British modernization only affected the cities; little change occurred in the villages. Taxation was high under British rule, and Britain invested little in developing the island's infrastructure.

Disillusionment with British rule and an increase in Greek nationalism on Cyprus resulted in Greek Cypriots demanding union with the Greek motherland, which had become independent with the demise of the Ottoman Empire at the end of World War I. Such demands led to riots in Nicosia in 1931. During World War II, Cyprus was not directly involved in the fighting, and the island gained from a boom in the economy.

Sir Garnet Wolseley (1833–1913), lieutenant general of the armies of Great Britain. In 1882 he seized the Suez Canal and secured Britain's trade with India.

ENOSIS

The end of World War II increased Greek Cypriot calls for *enosis* ("EH-noh-sees"), or union with Greece. Fearing marginalization, the Turkish minority, which was about 20% of the population, were hostile to this demand. Likewise, Turkey viewed the development of a potentially hostile state to its immediate south with some alarm. Britain was eager to retain Cyprus as part of NATO's military presence in the Middle East, and so discouraged *enosis*. In 1955 Greek guerrilla groups stepped up actions against the British, who were increasingly viewed as an occupation force. The National Organization for Cypriot Struggle (EOKA) bombed military buildings and attacked opponents of *enosis*, killing both British officers and Cypriots. Turkish Cypriots formed their own terror units, campaigning for *taksim* ("tahk-SIHM"), or division of the island. The British government drew up proposals for self-government, but the Greeks continued to pursue their nationalist aspirations. The two Cypriot communities became more polarized, and communal violence escalated into civil war in 1958.

With pressure from the United States, the Greek and Turkish governments came to an agreement in 1959 that was accepted by the British government and leaders of the Greek and Turkish Cypriot communities. Cyprus became an independent republic on August 16, 1960. The agreement stated that Cyprus would not unite with any other state or be subject to partition. Britain was to guarantee the island's sovereignty and military security in exchange for maintaining two military bases on the island. To prevent minority discrimination, Turks and Greeks were represented separately in the parliament, administration, police, and army.

This car was used to transport the EOKA leader, General G. Grivas Dighenis. It is one of the few reminders of the guerrilla group.

A UN observation point. While hostilities do occasionally break out at the "green line," the atmosphere has cooled considerably since the early days of partition. Today, the peacekeepers are more likely to suffer from boredom than anything dangerous.

INDEPENDENCE

The first independent elections were held in 1960, resulting in Archbishop Makarios winning 30 of the 35 Greek parliamentary seats, while Dr. Fazil Küçük and his supporters won all 15 Turkish-Cypriot seats. Makarios became Cyprus's first president, with Küçük as his deputy. In 1963 political disagreement arose, and fighting broke out between the two communities. Nicosia was divided—as it is today—by a ceasefire line, the "green line." Turkish Cypriots were reduced to living in a few urban enclaves and became reliant on relief packages for food and essentials.

The situation increased tensions between Turkey and Greece. By 1964, the United Nations had agreed to send a multinational peacekeeping force to replace British peacekeeping efforts. However, fighting intensified, and Turkish military aircraft intervened in some actions. Both Greece and Turkey began secretly sending regular troops to train and reinforce the warring factions.

In 1967 an incident led to Turkish threats to invade. The Greek military junta of the time agreed to withdraw their regular troops, and an uneasy peace was established. Turkish Cypriots were allowed to leave their enclaves and live and work where they pleased. Makarios was reelected president in 1968 and again in 1973. The Greek junta's relations with Makarios worsened because he was thought to be content with Cypriot independence, while many Greek Cypriots still sought union with the mainland. A struggle for power within the Greek nationalist community ensued.

THE GREEN LINE

Called the "green line" after a British soldier marked in green ink the dividing line between the Greek and Turkish sectors of Nicosia in 1963, the term is used today to describe the UN-monitored divide that runs through Nicosia. UN troops have been in Cyprus since 1964 to ensure the safety of the minority Turkish enclaves following a breakdown in ethnic relations. However, following the Turkish invasion in 1974, their task has become much bigger, monitoring the 125-mile (201-km) "Attila" line that divides the Greek South from the Turkish North. The "Attila" line was named after the Turkish military operation of 1974. Turkish and Greek Cypriot troops face each other across this buffer zone, while the no-man's-land in between is garrisoned by UN forces from UNFICYP, the UN Peacekeeping Force in Cyprus.

PARTITION

About 6,000 people died in the fighting in the summer of 1974.

On July 15, 1974, supporters of the nationalist cause, led by mainland Greek military officers, led a violent coup against Makarios and his republican supporters. Many left-wingers and republicans were murdered, and the presidential palace was left in ruins. The long-awaited *enosis* had been achieved overnight. The majority of the population, both Greek and Turkish, looked on helplessly, while Makarios escaped to the safety of the British base at Akrotiri. Nikos Sampson, a right-wing radical, was proclaimed president. However, Turkey would not tolerate the establishment of an overtly nationalist government that would potentially threaten their southern coast. Five days after the coup, Turkish troops landed on the northern beaches of the island, establishing a bridgehead around Kyrenia that linked to the Turkish sector of Nicosia. Vigorous fighting ensued.

Events in Greece created further confusion, with the fallen junta being replaced by a democratic government under Konstantinos Karamanlis on July 23. However, agreement was not reached between the guarantor powers, Greece, Britain, and Turkey until August 16, by which time the Turkish army controlled 37% of the island. As many as 165,000 Greeks fled the north of the island, leaving their possessions and property behind. Many lived in hastily-erected camps in southern Cyprus for months. Around 55,000 Turkish Cypriots were thought to have fled north to escape the bloody reprisals of Greek nationalists. In some villages, the entire adult male population was massacred by right-wing paramilitary groups.

GOVERNMENT

CYPRUS CURRENTLY has two governments. The Greek Cypriot-dominated Republic of Cyprus is still the legal government of Cyprus. The Turkish occupation of the northern portion of the island, however, undermines the republic's claims to be representative. Today, each community administers its own affairs, refusing to recognize the authority of the other's government.

The original constitution of 1960 provided that Cyprus be headed by a Greek president and a Turkish vice-president, elected for five-year terms by the whole electorate of the island. An elected House of Representatives of 50 seats was apportioned along ethnic lines—35 for Greek representatives, and 15 for Turkish Cypriot members. However, this constitution never inspired great confidence among Cypriots. Greek Cypriots sought closer relations with Greece, while Turkish Cypriots feared for their minority status. Attempts by Greek Cypriot politicians to change the constitution caused the ethnic schism that leaves Cyprus divided to this day.

Opposite: **British and Argentinian soldiers patrol the buffer zone. Britain, Greece, and Turkey are the official guarantors of the island's constitution and sovereignty. However, the long-standing enmity between Greece and Turkey has resulted in Cyprus becoming a symbol of this historical struggle and a potential flashpoint for conflict.**

Left: **Greek Cypriots' feelings of defiance shown through graffiti. The words mean, "Our borders are not here."**

Greek Cypriot women wave flags as they make their way to the Mia Milia checkpoint in Nicosia. Demonstrators, in a convoy of several hundred cars and motorcycles, protested in support of refugees who wanted to return to their former homes.

THE REPUBLIC OF CYPRUS

Where possible, as the official government of the island, the Republic of Cyprus still enforces the original constitution of 1960. However, since the withdrawal of Turkish Cypriot participation in government from 1964, the joint provisions in the constitution have been altered to ensure a non-communal, single representative government and administration. The president of the republic represents the republic at all official functions. A council of ministers holds executive power, controlling public services, monetary policy, foreign policy, and the drafting and passing of laws. The council is drawn from the House of Representatives. In 1985 the number of seats in the House expanded from 50 to 80, of which 56 are for Greek parties. Although 24 seats are reserved for Turkish parties, Turkish groups have not been represented since the beginning of the ethnic conflict.

Local government in the republic is at district, municipal, and village level. The government appoints district officers, while local councils and municipal mayors are elected.

POLITICAL PARTIES The oldest established party in the Republic of Cyprus is the Communist AKEL or Progressive Party of the Working People, founded in 1941. A pro-Moscow party, the AKEL achieved considerable success in the first 25 years of the republic, averaging 30% of the vote. Despite the breakup of the Soviet Union, it remains powerful in Greek Cypriot politics. The AKEL campaigns for a demilitarized, nonaligned, and independent Cyprus. The republic's other powerful party, the DISY or Democratic Rally party, seeks greater integration for Cyprus with Europe, especially through membership in the European Union. The party believes the European Union will help bring a peaceful solution to the problems of partition. Other parties include the EDEK or Socialist Party of Cyprus, the DIKO or Democratic Party, the EDE or United Democrats, and the NEO or New Horizons party.

In the national elections of 1996, the DISY won 20 seats in the House of Representatives, the AKEL 19 seats, DIKO 10 seats, EDEK five seats, and the EDE two seats. An even spread of support for the major parties ensures that coalition politics dominates, under the leadership of the president.

Glafkos Clerides waving to supporters shortly after casting his vote in the presidential election in February 1998. He won a second term in office.

PRESIDENTIAL ELECTIONS in February 1998 resulted in victory for Glafkos Clerides. In the first round of voting, Clerides and his party, the DISY, won 40% of the vote, as did his closest rival, George Iacovou, an independent candidate backed by the EDEK and DIKO. A runoff between the two contenders resulted in a narrow 51% to 49% victory for Clerides.

Turkish Cypriots beating a Greek Cypriot demonstrator in the buffer zone between north and south Cyprus on August 11, 1996. Turkish Cypriot police and UN soldiers stopped the violent clash between the Turkish and Greek Cypriots and saved this demonstrator's life.

THE TURKISH REPUBLIC OF NORTH CYPRUS

A provisional body, the Turkish Cypriot Federated State (1975–83), was established soon after the Turkish invasion to govern Turkish Cyprus. Following a stalemate in negotiations, the Turkish Republic of North Cyprus (TRNC) was declared in 1983, and the people approved a new constitution in a referendum in 1985. However, only Turkey recognizes the self-proclaimed state, and no countries have direct communication links or diplomatic relations with North Cyprus. All communication comes via the Turkish mainland. This isolation has forced the TRNC to rely on Turkey for much of its external infrastructure and trade. It also ensures that Turkey is a permanent and powerful player in TRNC politics.

The TRNC is a secular republic governed by a unicameral Legislative Assembly of 50 deputies. They are elected every five years by the people of TRNC. The country is run by a council of 10 ministers appointed from the Legislative Assembly by the president, on the advice of the prime minister.

RAUF DENKTASH

Denktash is the only person to ever have been elected president of the infant TRNC. As the former leader of the Turkish Cypriot Federated State, he has dominated the Turkish Cypriot political scene for more than 25 years. Born in Paphos, he is popular and trusted by Turkish Cypriots for his forthright and uncompromising representation of the Turkish Cypriot cause. The Cypriots see him as the best chance of a fair solution to the problems of partition.

The Turkish North has a similar system of justice as the Greek South. The highest court is the supreme court.

In the assembly elections in December 1998, the traditionally strong right-of-center National Unity Party (UBP) won 40.3% of the vote and the largest share of seats (24), making gains on its previous electoral showing in 1993. While no single party won overall control, the UBP entered into a coalition with the center-left Communal Liberation Party (TKP), which had won seven seats, to form the government. The UBP leader Dervis Eroglu remained as prime minister. The other parties in the assembly include the Republican Turkish Party (CTP), which is closely connected to mainland Turkish politics, and the Democratic Party (DP), the strongest opposition party with 13 seats.

THE PRESIDENT of the TRNC is appointed every five years by popular vote, independent of the Legislative Assembly. Rauf Denktash, standing as an independent, was elected president in 1995 for his third term.

THE LAW The legal codes of the republic are based on Roman law. The republic has a separate police force and legal administration. The government appoints the judges, but the judiciary is entirely independent of executive power. Courts exist at supreme and district level. District and assizes courts deal with civil and criminal cases, while the supreme court is the final court of appeal for cases from district courts and adjudication in constitutional and administrative law.

NEGOTIATIONS

Intercommunal negotiations have been an ongoing part of the Cypriot political scene even before independence. Since the Turkish invasion, Greek and Cypriot negotiators have met on numerous occasions in the hope of finding a solution to their differences. UN mediators have produced a plan in which Cyprus becomes an independent, bizonal republic—a proposal that both sides have broadly accepted in principle.

Nevertheless, over the years, negotiations have faced some stumbling blocks. The distribution of power between the two communities remains unclear. The Greek Cypriots campaign for a powerful central authority, which they, by virtue of their numbers, would probably control. Turkish Cypriots seek greater power for local districts, which would give them more autonomy. The Greeks seek freedom of movement within the whole federation, so Greek Cypriots would be able to return to their homes and

Cypriot president Clerides *(left)* shakes hands with Turkish Cypriot leader Denktash *(right)* as UN Secretary General Kofi Annan looks on. The meeting was part of on-going peace talks to reunite the island of Cyprus.

land in the north. Turkish Cypriots, however, reject this plan, fearing that they might quickly become a minority in their own sector. There is also the question of the huge number of Turks from the mainland who have settled in northern Cyprus since 1974. The Greek Cypriots do not recognize the settlers, who have perhaps increased the Turkish population by as many as 80,000. The Greek Cypriots demand the withdrawal of Turkish troops from the island and reject Turkey's role as a guarantor power. The Turkish Cypriots, on the other hand, want a Turkish military presence to ensure their security and political rights.

In 1992 the United Nations further developed its plan for a bizonal republic. This involved the two communities living in two separate zones with separate governments, while a weak, central government would be confined to joint decision-making on foreign policy, currency, and postal services. UN forces would remain to ensure the settlement was carried out peacefully, while there would be a drastic reduction in the numbers of Turkish troops. Furthermore, the Turkish zone would be reduced from 37% of the land to 28%, to align more proportionally with their smaller population. Property issues would also be settled and compensation paid. Still, it has been difficult to reach an agreement. Most Greeks believe the Turks should have no more than 25% of the land, while the Turkish Cypriots argue they should maintain at least 30%.

The presidency is also a contentious point. Although both sides agree to rotating Greek and Turkish presidents, in practice this may prove more difficult. Ironically, the chief negotiators, Denktash and Clerides, are longtime friends, both London-trained lawyers. Both have been involved in the intercommunal talks since the 1960s, but despite their knowledge of each other and the problem, a solution acceptable to all has yet to be found. Mediation in 1998 by American and Russian negotiators did not end the stalemate.

A.E. Yalman, editor of the Turkish newspaper, Vatan, *wrote in 1960: "Greece and Turkey have a common destiny. They are condemned either to be good neighbors, close friends, faithful allies—or to commit suicide together."*

ECONOMY

ALONG WITH MUCH OF the island's life, the Cypriot economy is divided between the north and the south. The economy of the Greek South is extremely prosperous, while the northern, Turkish economy is much smaller and poorer. While a Greek Cypriot earned an annual average of US$12,000 in 1997, earnings in the north were only a third as much. The economy of the south has averaged 4% growth per year for some time. The poorer Turkish North, however, averages growth of only half a percent each year. Three hundred thousand people work in the Republic of Cyprus; in the north, only 76,000 have jobs. Government revenues in the south reached almost US$3 billion in 1996, while in the north it was less than US$150 million. These economic differences, as much as any demographic, cultural, or ethnic factors, give the two sectors of the island contrasting appearances. As the republic develops into a wealthy country, the north is still in the early stages of economic development.

Opposite: **The port of Limassol is one of the fastest growing ports in Cyprus because of its excellent facilities.**

Left: **A farmer harvesting potatoes.**

Fishermen tending to their nets in a harbor in Ayia Napa. The fishing industry in Cyprus is not as important as one would expect for a Mediterranean island.

THE WEALTHY REPUBLIC

Between 1960 and 1974, before partition, Cyprus operated a successful, free-enterprise economy based on trade and agriculture that was the envy of its neighbors. Since 1974, the south has created an economic miracle. Much of its newly-generated wealth comes from the republic's service sector, which contributes 72% to the gross domestic product (GDP). The service industry employs 60% of the labor force, making it the most important sector in the Cypriot economy. Most services are related directly or indirectly to tourism, the lifeblood of the island's economy. Trade, communications, and offshore financial services are also an important part of the service sector. Because it is dependent on foreign revenue, the economy is vulnerable to fluctuations and changes in the economies of Europe and the Middle East. The standard of living in the republic remains higher than any of its Eastern Mediterranean neighbors.

In general, the economy of Greek Cyprus has remained healthy. Sustained low inflation has made the Cypriot government optimistic about their attempts to join the wealthy European Union trading block. Exports of commodities such as citrus fruit, potatoes, grapes, wine, cement, clothing, and shoes, reached US$1.4 billion in 1997. Its main export partners are Russia (17%), the United Kingdom (10%), Greece, and Germany. Imports reached a massive US$4 billion in 1997, consisting chiefly of consumer goods, petroleum, food, and machinery from the United States and the European Union. The republic helps offset this chronic trade deficit through its massive tourist earnings.

AGRICULTURE contributes only 5% of the republic's wealth each year, since most of the good arable land lies on the Mesaoria Plain near Famagusta and Morphou, in the Turkish North. Close to 10% of the workforce are employed in agriculture. The area around Paphos provides most of southern Cyprus's crops, including grapes, potatoes, tomatoes, watermelons, olives, and carobs. Citrus fruit is grown around Limassol. About 9.2 million gallons (35 million liters) of beer and 15.8 million gallons (60 million liters) of wine are produced each year, mainly for local consumption. Pigs and chickens are reared for consumption, cows and goats for their dairy products. About 70% of the agricultural produce is exported.

Packing oranges in a factory in Famagusta.

Strangely for an island, Cyprus has a small fishing industry and imports most of its fish and seafood. This is chiefly caused by the shortage of plankton in the island's waters. Plankton are tiny organisms that fish feed on for nutrients. Small fishing boats go for sole, whitebait, and red mullet, while commercial vessels look for swordfish.

An asbestos mine in Amiandos, on the eastern face of the Troodos Mountains. Copper was once the island's best known resource. Over the years, however, copper production has rapidly declined, and the production of asbestos, chrome, and gypsum has taken precedence.

INDUSTRY, which includes manufacturing, mining, and construction, contributes 23% to the republic's total earnings each year and employs a quarter of the workforce. Natural resources are few, thus industrial development is limited. The manufacturing industry produces piping and cement from asbestos and gypsum. Bricks, tiles, clothing, footwear, and machinery are also produced.

FINANCE AND BANKING constitute a significant part of Cyprus's service sector, contributing 17% of the country's wealth each year and employing 8% of the workforce. This includes offshore banking—as many as 22,000 offshore enterprises are registered in Cyprus, including insurance companies, real estate firms, and consulting firms. The Cypriot government, promoting the incentives of a favorable tax system and reliable infrastructure, has had considerable success in positioning Cyprus as an ideal base for offshore businesses, especially those wishing to do business in the Middle East. Most offshore companies come from the United Kingdom, Germany, and Russia.

TURKISH REPUBLIC OF NORTH CYPRUS

The north's diplomatic isolation from the international community has resulted in the TRNC's heavy reliance on Turkey for external trade and investment. The country's economy and infrastructure have been integrated into that of the mainland, and the Turkish currency, the Turkish lira, has become legal tender in the north. To compensate for the economy's frailty, Turkey has for years provided aid to nearly every sector of the TRNC economy, including tourism, industry, and education.

The economy relies heavily on agriculture and government services, which together employ almost half the workforce. Like the south, the service sector constitutes a massive 65% of the economy. Much of this is concentrated in state administration, and less is dedicated to tourism, financial services, and real estate development.

Trade is also a significant sector of the economy. Exports of citrus fruit, potatoes, and textiles to the United Kingdom and Turkey reached US$71 million in 1996, while imports, consisting mainly of food, minerals, chemicals, and machinery, reached US$330 million. Most imported goods come from Turkey (53%) and the United Kingdom (14%). A low tariff barrier for Turkish goods and the superior development of the Turkish industry means that Turkish imports remain cheap and more competitive compared to local products. This, and the use of the Turkish lira, has led to high levels of inflation imported from the mainland. These factors have limited the growth of small-scale manufacturing in the TRNC.

A young girl helps her parents separate olives from the leaves.

AGRICULTURE contributes 12% to the north's wealth each year. It employs nearly a quarter of the working population and is an essential foreign currency earner for north Cyprus. Most of the island's crops are grown on the Mesaoria Plain, including olives, potatoes, wheat, barley, and tobacco. Guzelyurt, an area around Morphou, is the market garden of Cyprus, where oranges and other citrus fruit are grown in abundance. Fishing and growing tobacco are the main activities on the remote Karpas Peninsula. The main fishing ports are Bogaz and Kumyali. Animal farming is primarily chickens, sheep, and goats.

INDUSTRY, including manufacturing and construction, contributes 23% to GDP. Most industrial output is absorbed by the domestic market. The growth of local industry has been hampered by difficulties in reaching international markets, an inability to attract new investment, and the competition of cheap imports from Turkey. Clothing, cartons, and processed food products, such as juices and animal feed, are the chief exports. Construction constitutes 5% of the economy, in part a consequence of the expanding tourist industry.

A power station in Kyrenia.

ENERGY Power supply is one area in which the two communities have managed to cooperate. Since most of the island's water reserves lie in the north of Cyprus, the republic, in exchange for water, provides the TRNC with most of its electricity supplies. A large portion of the needed petroleum products are imported.

THE TOURIST DOLLAR

Tourism has been Cyprus's biggest and most important growth industry since the partition in 1983, with the southern portion of the island now receiving more than two million visitors a year. Visitors, coming especially from Britain, Germany, and Scandinavia, swamp Cyprus from May to October, outnumbering the local population. The beaches around Limassol, the resorts of Ayia Napa and Protaris at Cape Greco in the far southeastern corner, and the historical town of Paphos in the west offer numerous first-class hotels and tourist facilities for those seeking sun and sand.

These resorts have mostly been developed since partition. Forest stations have been built to accommodate tourists in the Troodos Mountains, and numerous forest trails have been developed. The boom in the tourist industry has had positive consequences for the republic's construction industry, with the building of many hotels, apartments, and restaurants. Tourist centers such as Ayia Napa, for example, were insignificant rural villages some 20 years ago, but with the explosion of tourism, have developed into a vast complex of hotels, restaurants, bars, and recreational facilities. The ancient sites of Curium, Citium, Amathus, Khirokitia, and Paphos are an added attraction. While tourism has made the south rich, many people bemoan the environmental and aesthetic effects of large numbers of square hotels and apartment blocks in overdeveloped areas such as Ayia Napa and the beaches east of Limassol.

TOURISM North Cyprus has a far less developed tourist industry than the south, but as a consequence has grown in popularity because of its reputation for unspoiled natural beauty. In recent years, as many as 360,000 tourists have visited northern Cyprus annually, and the number is rising. Of these, only a fraction come from northern Europe. Most come from Turkey and the Arab world. Since the late 1970s, North Cyprus has been advertised as a shopping destination for Turkish tourists. Most tourists still stay in hotels in and around the beaches of Kyrenia and Famagusta. Tourist earnings contribute more than 60% of the TRNC's total foreign earnings. Increasingly, Turkish Cypriots who fled the fighting in the 1960s and '70s are returning from abroad to invest in the tourist industry. In recent years, many new hotels have been built.

TRANSPORTATION

North and south Cyprus are served by separate transportation systems, and there are no services linking the two parts of the island. The Republic of Cyprus has 6,300 miles (10,136 km) of road, while the TRNC has 1,500 miles (2,414 km) of road. Modern, four-lane highways link Nicosia with Larnaca and Limassol, and Limassol to Paphos. However, a substantial part of the road system in the rural and mountainous areas is unpaved. An extensive bus service allows Cypriots in the rural areas to travel to the main towns and cities. The roads in north Cyprus are less developed than the south and are far less busy. Cypriots drive on the left, a relic of British colonial administration. There is no functioning railroad.

The main international sea ports in the south are Limassol and Larnaca, both constructed after the Turkish invasion. In the north, Famagusta and

Erkan International Airport is not recognized by the International Air Transport Association (IATA) and is considered an illegal port of entry by the Greek Cypriot authorities.

Kyrenia still operate sea traffic with the Turkish mainland. Limassol and Larnaca act as transshipment terminals for cargo going to and from the Eastern Mediterranean. Today, Larnaca mainly functions as a berth for oil tankers. Cyprus is ranked one of the world's top bases for merchant shipping—3.86 million tons (3.5 million metric tons) of cargo are handled in Larnaca and Limassol each year. Until the Turkish invasion, Famagusta was the island's most important sea port, handling 80% of all sea traffic. Today, Famagusta only serves the Turkish region. Vehicle ferries ply a trade between Famagusta and Mersin in southern Turkey, and in the summer season, passenger and car ferries also run to Kyrenia.

The international airport in Nicosia has been closed since the Turkish invasion. Consequently, a new international airport was built at Larnaca, with connections to most European and Middle Eastern destinations, and links to North America. A smaller but busy airport has also been built at Paphos, mainly to deal with tourist flights from Europe. At the height of the tourist season, dozens of flights fly into these airports everyday. Cyprus Airways is the national carrier, owned jointly by the government and local businesses. Turkish Cyprus's chief international link is Erkan, a small airport east of Nicosia. Only two air carriers fly scheduled flights to Erkan—Turkish Airlines and Cyprus Turkish Airlines. Chartered flights carrying tourists from Britain and other parts of northern Europe fly to Erkan but have to touch down in Turkey first. A second airport was also opened at Lefkoniko, north of Famagusta, in 1986.

A local bus that serves a dual purpose—ferrying passengers and transporting goods.

CYPRIOTS

THE OFFICIAL POPULATION of Cyprus was 775,000 in 1997, although this does not take into account the large number of officially unrecognized Turkish settlers who have arrived since 1974. Greek Cypriots make up 78% of the official population, Turkish Cypriots constitute 18%, while Maronites, Armenians, Greeks, and other Europeans contribute 4%. The Maronites, Armenians, and Greeks are classified as native Cypriots. Nearly 80% of the population live in the prosperous Republic of Cyprus.

Both Greek and Turkish Cypriots emigrated in large numbers following independence in 1960 and again after the Turkish invasion in 1974. It is estimated that there are as many people of Cypriot descent living abroad as on the island itself. The majority went to the United Kingdom, and as many as 100,000 Greek Cypriots live in London. Other English-speaking countries such as Australia, the United States, and Canada have also been popular destinations.

Opposite: **A young Cypriot girl. Children form a quarter of the total population.**

Left: **Cypriots love to gather in taverns with friends.**

One of the rare occasions when Turkish and Greek Cypriots dance together during a festival in front of the Ledra Palace Hotel in the buffer zone. The UN mission in Cyprus held the festival celebrations in the buffer zone in an attempt to ease tensions between the two sides.

COMMUNAL STRENGTH, ETHNIC DIVISIONS

Most Cypriots define themselves in terms of their ethnic identity, and "Cypriot" is always prefixed with the qualification of "Greek" or "Turkish." For many centuries, Cypriots lived in ethnically-mixed villages, and by appearance it was impossible to tell the two communities apart. Nevertheless, despite 400 years of largely peaceful cohabitation, cultural and religious differences resulted in little genuine mixing between the two communities. Greek Cypriots remain culturally oriented toward Greece, speak Greek, and practice the Greek Orthodox religion, while Turkish Cypriots speak Turkish and practice the Islamic religion. The religious differences in particular have made intermarriage difficult and unlikely.

Since the partition of the island, the differences have become more pronounced, while the movement of refugees in both directions has meant coexistence is virtually unheard of. While history has created the schism in the Cypriot community, current attitudes further entrench the divide. Ethnic nationalism is rife—Turkish flags flutter above many buildings in the north of the island, just as the Greek cross of St. Andrew adorns every church and public building in the south. The Turks are clearly oriented toward the Turkish mainland, while the Greeks look toward Athens and Europe. Mutual mistrust has hardened as time passes, and linguistic and cultural barriers are increasing. Few Greek Cypriots now speak Turkish, and the only Turkish Cypriots who speak Greek are a few older people who worked for Greek businesses before 1974.

While most Turkish and Greek Cypriots moved to their allotted sides of the Attila line following the division of the island in 1974, some small ethnic enclaves exist on both sides of the border. In the north, 500 to 600 Greek Cypriots still live around the village of Dipkarpas on the Karpas Peninsula, the residue of some 20,000 Greeks who had lived there before the Turkish invasion. Once a week, UN blue beret forces deliver food and mail from Greek Nicosia; relatives from Greek Cyprus are intermittently also allowed to visit. Only two elementary schools still operate, and children above 11 seeking secondary education have to go to the south, with no automatic right to return and live in their village.

Surprisingly, one bi-ethnic village remains on the island, an example of how Cypriots lived before the partition. Situated where the Attila line buffer zone meets the British base at Dhekelia, the village of Pyla remains a vestige of the past, a perfect microcosm of the island before 1974. Greeks (67%) and Turks (33%) live in proximity but not together, socializing in separate coffeehouses and attending separate communal schools.

A young boy in the town of Paphos, adding to the donkey's load. His father is harvesting crops.

A knife seller in a market in Nicosia.

GREEK CYPRIOTS

Through the centuries, Greek Cypriots have maintained their Greek identity. The retention of the Greek language and the establishment of the Greek Orthodox religion through the independent Church of Cyprus, have become the twin bastions of the Greek Cypriot identity. The Greeks have clung so fiercely to their roots because they were subject to constant invasion and conquest by foreign powers in the past. The Ottoman occupation, and the more recent threat from Turkey, have led the Greek Cypriot population to assert their identity even more firmly than they would if they did not feel threatened.

Almost all (99%) Greek Cypriots live in the south, and most have been abroad at some time or another. For those who can afford it, overseas education is popular, especially in Greece and Britain. Most Greek Cypriots speak at least a smattering of English. Because of this, Greek Cypriots think of themselves as Europeans, despite their geographical proximity and historical links to the Middle East.

TURKISH CYPRIOTS

Many Turkish Cypriots are descendants of the mainland Turks who remained on the island after the Ottoman conquest in the 16th century. During that period, religion rather than ethnicity was the determining civic factor. Thus many of today's Turkish Cypriots do not trace their lineage to Turkey, but to a variety of sources, including the Balkans and Africa.

Since 1974, more mainland Turks have settled with their families in Cyprus to work on farms. These settlers are given TRNC citizenship if they remain on the island for more than five years. Turkish immigration has reinforced the Turkish identity of the north and created a stronger relationship with Turkey. However, social tensions have built up over the years. The Turkish Cypriots think that the mainlanders are increasingly controlling the economy and dictating the north's relations with the international community. They also believe that the steady influx of mainland Turks is slowly diluting the Turkish Cypriot identity, making them more Anatolian in character.

53

TRADITIONAL DRESS

Traditional dress is an important aspect of Cyprus's traditional culture, although today, it is only worn on festive occasions. Cotton and silk, and a blend of the two called *itare* ("IH-tahr-eh"), are the main materials used. Silkworms are bred on the island and most materials are woven in the home. Traditionally, the best festival dress are associated with marriage practices, especially dowry ceremonies. Items worn by the bridegroom, such as a silk handkerchief, are offered as a gift to his fiancée.

Compared to the dress of their mainland Greek compatriots, Greek Cypriot clothes are simpler and more uniform. For women, two styles are most popular. The *karpasitiko* ("karp-ahs-IHT-ih-koh") includes a white, long-sleeved dress with a high, round neck. Full white trousers, either plain or embroidered, are worn underneath the dress. A tight-fitting, long coat with decorated sleeves is worn over the top. The front of the coat is low-cut, to reveal the dress. On her head, a woman wears an embroidered white or colored handkerchief, either draped or folded. The other popular choice is a black velvet, long-sleeved jacket worn over a long cotton shirt with a long, checked or striped skirt. A red fez or white handkerchief is worn on the head. Low-heeled, black shoes are worn with both dress. The man's traditional dress includes a white, long-sleeved shirt and full, baggy black trousers tucked into black boots. A black sash is tied around the waist, and a black, embroidered vest is worn over the shirt. A small, black cap is worn on the back of the head.

For Turkish Cypriots, traditional dress derived from mainland Turkey is worn on festive occasions. Men will wear a red fez, and parts of the body are stained with red henna. Religion and custom decree that no hair should be seen, so both men and women wear a headdress. Until recently, women covered their faces with veils or draped scarves. The basic dress has remained the same for many centuries—baggy trousers, called *shalvar* ("shahl-VAHR"), are worn by the women, along with a vest or a high-necked, calf-length jacket. Men also wear the *shalvar*, most often colored black or blue. Short, embroidered vests, called *cepken* ("chep-KEHN"), are worn over high-necked, white shirts. Leather sandals with turned up toes are worn by both men and women.

OTHER PEOPLES

Inevitably, because of the island's checkered and turbulent history, many other people have settled in Cyprus over the centuries. While most have assimilated into the Greek or Turkish communities, a few groups, such as the Maronites and Armenians, retain a distinct identity.

MARONITES are an Arab people from Lebanon who practice a form of Catholicism. They first came to Cyprus with the Lusignan Crusaders in the 12th century, serving as archers against the Arabs. Saint Maron, a Syrian hermit of the late 4th century, and later Saint John Maron, the patriarch of Antioch from A.D. 657–707, are the founders of the Maronite religion.

Korucam (Turkish "Kormacit"), north of Morphou, is the Cypriot Maronite capital, though only a few hundred Maronites still live in the village. They worship at a church in the village, Ayios Georgios, without interference from the Turkish authorities. Since partition, most Maronites have moved to the south to seek a better life, and the community in Korucam is steadily declining. Maronites speak their native tongue, which is a dialect of Arabic mixed with many Greek and Turkish words.

ARMENIANS Trade links have existed with Armenia since ancient times. Armenians first arrived in Cyprus in the 6th century A.D., a consequence of struggles between the Byzantines and Arabs. When Armenia was brought under the influence of the Byzantine Empire, as many as 10,000 Armenians were forcibly settled in Cyprus by the Byzantine emperors to work the land. As fellow Christians, the Armenians had few problems assimilating into Greek Cypriot culture. However, with opportunities to emigrate to North America, Europe, and Australia, the Armenian community remains small in Cyprus, numbering just a few thousand today.

Despite attempts by Muslim caliphs and the Ottoman Turks to subjugate and absorb the Maronites, today they constitute one of the major religious-ethnic groups in modern Lebanon.

EXPATRIATES

Cyprus has a notable expatriate population, mostly people from northern Europe who have chosen to retire or set up a business there. Holiday homes and villas have been built in many parts of southern Cyprus to cater to the influx of people seeking to enjoy the island's dry, warm climate and relaxed atmosphere. The Cypriot government's favorable tax concessions and improvements in the infrastructure have helped this development.

As many as 5,000 British nationals have settled in Cyprus, mostly in the south around Limassol. Some own bars and restaurants around the popular tourist areas of Limassol, Ayia Napa, and Paphos, while some operate offshore businesses or are connected with the British military. Many of these people have come to Cyprus to retire in a country that retains strong economic and cultural links with Britain. Britain maintains military bases in Cyprus, where English is widely spoken. Many Germans and Scandinavians have also chosen to make Cyprus their home. There are also many Lebanese, Arab, Iranian, Russian, and Serbian entrepreneurs living in Limassol and Nicosia, usually running offshore banking and other services linked to interests in the Middle East and Eastern Europe.

The British military bases near Limassol and Larnaca give the two towns a very British feel at times, especially during the tourist season. The bases of Akrotiri and Dhekelia are miniature Britains, with pubs, housing developments, golf courses, and military hospitals to serve the military community. Most British soldiers are well-behaved and appreciated for the money that they spend in the bars, restaurants, and clubs on the island, but fights between soldiers and locals, and soldiers and tourists occasionally occur. The conviction of three British servicemen for the rape of a Danish tour guide in 1996 caused distrust and resentment. Although such incidents are rare, it fuels tensions between the British military and the local population. In 1996 Cypriots held demonstrations against the British presence.

In the north, foreign presence is far less noticeable. In the early and mid-20th century, the town of Kyrenia was a popular retirement place for former colonial officials. Before the Turkish invasion, some 2,000, mainly British expatriates, lived in Kyrenia. By 1976, most had fled, and only 200 remained. With the establishment of peace and the growth of tourism, this number has increased in the last 10 years.

LIFESTYLE

FOR MANY CENTURIES, despite the country's exposure to varied foreign influences, the traditional Cypriot lifestyle did not alter much. The island's conquerors generally remained aloof from the Cypriot peasants, allowing them to get on with their lives. However, in the south, with increased prosperity and Westernization, lifestyle has changed dramatically in the last 30 years. This is a consequence of British influence and the south's gradual integration with the European economy.

More young Cypriots choose to leave their traditional villages and live in cities or even go abroad, where there are greater opportunities. Cyprus has a young population—nearly half are under 30. These demographic changes have potentially far-reaching consequences for the Cypriot way of life. The attitudes and experiences of the young, which are markedly different from their elders, are increasingly dominant. While the island has virtually full employment on both sides of the border, a lack of varied career opportunities still persuades many young Cypriots to leave.

The Cypriot lifestyle remains relaxed compared to many neighboring countries. Cypriots tend to be calmer in their reactions to life's irritations, and the pace of life in cities like Nicosia and Famagusta is far more laid-back than in either Athens or Istanbul. The average life expectancy in Cyprus is 76 years (78 years for women and 74 years for men). The crime rate is extremely low on both sides of the divide. Major offenses, such as assault or murder, occur rarely, while theft is virtually unheard of.

Above: **Selling ice-cream in one of the streets of Lefkara.**

Opposite: **A Cypriot woman hanging out cheese.**

VILLAGE LIFE

Before the Turkish invasion in 1974, there were over 600 villages in Cyprus. The village constituted the core of Cypriot life for both Greeks and Turks. In bicommunal villages, Muslim minarets and church bell-towers formed the same skyline. Today, there are only 300 inhabited villages where the traditional rural lifestyle remains. Despite this decline, village life remains important to many older Cypriots and is inextricably linked to notions of Cypriot identity.

The typical Cypriot village consists of a series of narrow roads and tracks linking outlying farms to the village. The village itself is centered around the village square. In the square there will probably be a church or mosque, depending on whether the village is Greek or Turkish, a coffeehouse, and a number of stores. Men tend to begin work at dawn, often finishing their farm chores by midday. Irrigating the crops is an essential daily activity on this sun-parched island, and is the difference between success and failure for the farmer. Stocks of water and underground

RURAL EXODUS

Since the 1960s, there has been a very pronounced drift from village to town all over Cyprus, a trend accelerated by the ethnic conflicts and partition of the island. Cypriots are traditionally a rural people. Before 1931, only 22% of Cypriots lived in a town, and until 1974, more than half the population lived in villages. Today, in the south, approximately 70% of the people live in urban areas. The average age of the inhabitants in some of the more remote villages in the Troodos Mountains is 60 years, suggesting that many villages may become deserted in the near future. In the 1960s it was common for village people to commute to the towns to work, since most villages were within an hour's travel to one of the six towns. However, a series of factors has led to a rapid expansion of the towns. They include the need for new housing created by the refugees who settled in Cyprus following the Turkish invasion, the increased modernization of life, especially in the south, the massive building boom, and the development of the coastal-based tourist industry.

Expectations for Cypriots have risen sharply. Apart from the influence of tourist development, the harsh village life has led many young Cypriots to look for better lives in the towns. Greater educational opportunities and a higher standard of living encouraged younger Cypriots to seek more than the simple rural life of earlier generations. The Paphos district, for example, had been a rural backwater offering few opportunities. During the 1960s and 1970s, many Cypriots from the district migrated to other regions, since Paphos had limited work on the plantations along the coast. The Turks left after the 1974 invasion, further reducing the population by one quarter, leaving many former Turkish villages deserted. Most of the young people work as hotel receptionists, bar staff, and cooks, suggesting that while the district is now prospering, vital, traditional links with the rural way of life are being lost.

The Cypriot government has introduced many plans to improve agricultural life and rural infrastructure, such as irrigation projects and building local schools, in an attempt to promote the village lifestyle and protect the rural heritage. The new inhabitants of many villages are often wealthy outsiders who have no particular link to the district. However, they are poor cultural substitutes for the communities that have once existed.

reservoirs are constantly monitored. The coffeeshop is the fulcrum of the village for the men, where news and gossip are exchanged. Women are excluded from this activity, and are usually found either looking after the family or working in the fields. Even old women will help bring in the harvest and tend the livestock. Nevertheless, life is not wholly one of toil for Cypriot women. They often sit in shady backstreets to embroider, knit, and gossip. On the weekends, villages burst into activity. The extended family gathers to eat and exchange news, and the taverns and coffeeshops are at their liveliest. During festival times, processions, feasting, music, and dancing transform the village, bringing it to life.

COFFEEHOUSES

The coffeehouse, or *kahve* ("kah-VEH") in Turkish, *kapheneia* ("gahf-EHN-ee-ah") in Greek, is a permanent and defining aspect of the life of the island, especially in the villages. The center of village life, coffeehouses are very male-dominated establishments. Sitting in the coffeehouses and discussing the problems of the world, be it money, soccer, weather, or politics, is the favorite pastime of most Cypriot men. Commonly located on the village square, the

coffeehouse provides a public meeting place for the men of the community to discuss local issues, relax, and exchange gossip. Men will often while away many hours playing backgammon or card games. Increasingly, coffeeshops are also equipped with television, though it is generally turned on only for soccer games or movies. Before partition, most villages had two coffeehouses, one for the Turkish community and one for the Greek, but today this is no longer necessary.

Hospitality is the hallmark of the coffeehouse, and strangers hesitating at the door will usually be invited in. The coffeehouses are usually open all day, and often the men will gather there early in the morning before starting work for a quick cup. At the end of the day, they will also settle down at the coffeehouse for another cup of coffee. Coffeehouses sell mainly coffee and cold drinks, including beer and spirits. The coffee is normally very strong and drunk in small quantities, accompanied by a glass of water to wash it down. In the evening, the men might switch to brandy. In small, isolated villages, the coffeehouse even serves as a local store and post office.

A refusal to accept a host's hospitality is considered extremely rude.

HOSPITALITY

Hospitality is one of the cornerstones of the Cypriot way of life, and Cypriots are usually generous and gracious hosts. Even the poorest peasant feels bound to honor their guests as lavishly as they can afford to. Turkish Cypriots are far less exposed to foreigners than their Greek counterparts, and consequently treat guests, or in Turkish *misafir* ("mihs-ah-FEER"), with lavish cordiality and generosity. Typically, Turkish Cypriots will ply their guests with food and drink, especially coffee.

HOUSING

The traditional rural dwellings of Cyprus have maintained the same character for many centuries. Most of them are functional, as farmers believe that dwellings should only be big enough to accommodate their inhabitants, while the surrounding land should stretch as far as the eye can see. The houses are built around a courtyard, with a beehive-shaped clay oven in the center.

In the towns of the south, modern dwellings are two-story, airy buildings built in a style found throughout the Mediterranean. The center of Limassol and Larnaca are dominated by high-rise buildings, an increasingly familiar sight throughout Cyprus. Many wealthy Cypriots and expatriates build villas for themselves on the edge of the towns. The urban areas have rapidly expanded, swallowing up many smaller villages in the process.

Usually made from mud and clay bricks, traditional rural dwellings represent a microcosm of Cypriot history, having been constructed partly with stone plundered from ancient Greek and Roman dwellings, and from Venetian fortifications.

Many modern houses have an attached plot of land that the parents save to build a house for their daughter and her prospective husband.

For Greek Cypriot weddings, the church service is held on a Sunday, because any other day is considered unlucky.

FAMILY AND MARRIAGE

The family has always been an important part of Cypriot society, be it the Greek community or the Turkish Cypriot community. When Cypriots speak of their families, they do not only mean immediate relations; the family circle extends to second cousins and further. Families are a great source of support and pride, and kinship links are kept religiously. Family members are obliged to help each other at any time and in any way possible, including lending money, helping with employment or establishing business contacts, building homes, or finding suitable marriage partners.

Cypriot parents are willing to sacrifice a great deal for their children, and no expense is spared in ensuring that they attain a high level of education, especially the boys. As far as possible, girls are shielded from the harsher realities of modern life, and parents keep a watchful eye for harmful male influences. Even today, many Cypriot girls lead very sheltered lives. Traditionally, the women's role was strictly circumscribed, and she was expected to remain in the house. If seen out with a male who was not her official fiancé, her virtue was considered compromised, and she might consequently have difficulties finding a male suitor.

Traditionally, marriages are arranged in Cyprus, and while this custom is still practiced, it is more common now for the young to choose their own partners. After marriage, women are expected to look after the house and rear children, and leisure activities are limited to watching television and visiting relatives. While these restrictions are not as widespread in modern

Cyprus as in the past, much of this morality lingers, and women have to be careful of their behavior.

Men, on the other hand, as the breadwinners and heads of the household, are allowed, and expected, to pursue their own entertainment and pleasure. Cyprus is still very much a male-dominated society, and women are characterized in conservative terms. While women rarely venture into male-dominated professions, such as law and politics, many women today have paid jobs. Greater economic independence has helped liberate them from the restrictions of traditional, sex-designated roles. Although divorce statistics are rising, marriage is still the life choice of the vast majority of young Cypriots. Homosexuality is illegal on both sides of the dividing line, and gay life is virtually nonexistent in the island's tight-knit, family-oriented society.

WEDDING EXPENSES: THE DOWRY

Traditionally, fathers choose their daughters' marriage partners. In doing so, they bear responsibility for the future happiness of their children. This acceptance of responsibility is expressed through the giving of a dowry, or gift, to the daughter to accompany her in the marriage. The dowry is often substantial. It is traditional and desirable to provide a home for the newlyweds, which is also a useful method of passing on property from one generation to the next. The bigger the gift, the more favorable the girl's marriage prospects, since a more generous dowry will attract wealthier and better suitors. Traditionally, it is considered a disgrace for a daughter to remain unmarried, and so fathers will build a house at almost any cost to avoid the shame; few suitors would be interested in a girl without property. Poorer families may have to stretch the construction over many years, while the rich will build property as early as possible. Although preparing a dowry is an enormous expense to the parents, this is considered the first priority for the family, even at the expense of the son's education.

The Greek Cypriot wedding ceremony retains many traditional features. If it is a village wedding, the whole community will be invited to attend, as well as all family members and friends, whether near or far. If the wedding is in a town, an announcement will be placed in the local newspaper inviting guests, which usually means a very large crowd.

EDUCATION

In the south, elementary education is compulsory and free for all children from age 5 to 12. Free secondary education lasts for a further six years. This includes three years at a gymnasium and three noncompulsory years in high school. Less than 2,000 students attend classes at the University of Cyprus, which was opened in 1992. A further 6,000 students study at 30 other institutions of higher learning across the island. An education overseas is still the choice of many Cypriots, with 8,000 to 9,000 going abroad each year, especially to Britain and Greece.

In the Turkish North, preschool and elementary education are free and compulsory for all children from age 5 to 11. Secondary education, for 12- to 18-year-olds, is available at high schools and vocational colleges. Secondary education is free but not compulsory. Higher education is state-provided. Universities have been established in Nicosia, Famagusta, and Lefke. The Eastern Mediterranean University near Famagusta is North Cyprus's largest university.

WORK AND WELFARE

Working hours throughout the island revolve around the Mediterranean siesta. Typically, shops are open from 8 a.m. to 1 p.m. and 2:30 to 5:30 p.m. in the winter, and 7:30 a.m. to 1 p.m. and 4 p.m. to 7 p.m. in the summer. The Cypriot government operates a comprehensive social insurance program covering all working adults and their dependants. Benefits from the program cover unemployment, sickness, maternity leave, injury at work, and an old-age pension. All contributions to the program are income-related. Workers are protected against unjust dismissal. Unemployment is low in the Greek portion of Cyprus, averaging less than 3%.

In the north, while official statistics suggest unemployment at an extremely low 2%–3%, there is considerable underemployment, particularly in farming. Most people work, but do not have quite enough to ensure prosperity. As a result of regular high inflation, a minimum wage is fixed by law for all occupations and determined by a commission including the government and employers. A cost-of-living allowance is also paid to offset the effects of high inflation. However, while government bodies pay the allowance regularly, private companies do not. This has led to public sector employees becoming wealthier than their private sector counterparts. Although the north-south border is officially closed, it is estimated that 2,000 Turkish workers travel to work in the south each day through the British base in Dhekelia. While some work on the base, many travel farther to work on building sites in the south.

A Turkish Cypriot artisan at work. Only one in three Turkish Cypriots belongs to a trade union, mainly in the farming, teaching, government, and blue-collar sectors.

RELIGION

RELIGION IN CYPRUS reflects both the island's complicated history and its ethnic composition. There are Muslim mosques, Orthodox churches, Armenian churches, and Catholic cathedrals, an indication of the many faiths that have over the years found adherents in Cyprus. The vast majority of Greek Cypriots follow the Orthodox faith, while Turkish Cypriots practice Islam. In the republic, 93% of the population follow the Cypriot version of the Orthodox faith, while 1.5% are Maronites. The remainder are Anglicans and Muslims. In north Cyprus, 98% of the people are Muslims, the remainder Maronites, Orthodox Greek Cypriots, and followers of the Armenian Apostolic faith. Despite a wide belief in religion, observers have noted a decline in religious observance. Islam has not practiced with great fervor, and some Cypriot Muslims have a relaxed attitude toward mosque attendance.

The partition of the island has had the result of segregating Cyprus into an Islamic north and an Orthodox south. Only two churches remain open in north Cyprus: Ayios—the Greek word for "Saint"—Mamas near Morphou and Ayios Varnavas near Famagusta. Many other churches in the north have either been converted to mosques or museums, or desecrated by the Turkish army. South of the partition line, a mosque still operates in each of the cities of Larnaca, Limassol, and Nicosia to serve the needs of the republic's sizeable population of Arabs, Iranians, and the remaining Turkish Cypriots. The other mosques, left empty since the Muslim migration to the north, are locked and maintained by the government.

Above: **The Lala Mustapha Pasha Mosque in Famagusta.**

Opposite: **St. Anthony's church in Paphos.**

Followers entering the Kykko Monastery. The proudest and richest of all Cyprus monasteries, this church has, since its construction in the 19th century, been burned to the ground several times. However, its most precious possession, an icon of the Virgin Mary, has miraculously come through all the fires unscathed.

THE CHURCH OF CYPRUS

The huge number of Orthodox churches throughout the island and the beauty of the frescoes and icons inside the churches bear testimony to the island's strong Orthodox Christian traditions. The majority of Cyprus's Greeks are Orthodox Christians, a part of the Eastern Orthodox faith that is dominant in Greece, Russia, and much of Eastern Europe. However, Cypriots have their own independent church, the Orthodox Church of Cyprus. While similar in practice to the Greek Orthodox Church, the Church of Cyprus is not under the authority of an external patriarch. In A.D. 488 the Byzantine emperor Zeno granted this privilege to Archbishop Anthemius. Since the 18th century, the Cypriot clergy have played a prominent social and political role on the island, mainly as a result of the Ottoman style of rule that gave both secular and religious authority to the clergy. Consequently, the archbishop of Cyprus was also given the title of "ethnarch," or national leader of the Greek community. The archbishop is elected by representatives of the towns and villages of Cyprus.

SAINT BARNABAS

One of the island's most famous monasteries is named after Saint Barnabas, companion of Saint Paul, and one of those responsible for bringing Christianity to Cyprus. Barnabas was born in Salamis and is revered as the founder of the Cypriot church. He was martyred by stoning in A.D. 75, having raised the ire of the Salamis Jewish community.

The discovery of Barnabas's bones buried beneath a carob tree on the Mesaoria Plain in the late fifth century provides the Church of Cyprus a foundation on which to claim its ecclesiastical independence. Following the unearthing of the apostle's remains, the archbishop of Cyprus set off to Constantinople to request that the Cypriot church be granted an autonomous status. The Byzantine emperor Zeno agreed, persuaded by the gift of the original copy of the Gospel of Saint Matthew, supposedly handwritten by Barnabas and found clasped in the dead saint's arms. The tomb of Barnabas is at the Monastery of Apostolos Varnavas (Barnabas), situated north of Famagusta. Cypriots of all faiths still revere the location.

Orthodox worship is highly visual, and ritual plays an important role. Orthodox churches are richly decorated with religious art, including icons, frescoes, murals, and ecclesiastical vessels. The intention is to provide strong visual encouragement for the worshippers, stimulating faith and piety. Icons are positioned around the inside of most churches, and walls are covered with frescoes depicting religious events and symbolizing religious ideas. An iconostasis—a highly decorated partition that divides the sanctuary from the rest of the church—is also a part of Orthodox worship. The congregation looks into the sanctuary through doorways in the iconostasis. On each side of the doorways are icons representing Christ, the Virgin Mary, the four Evangelists, and the Last Supper. Symbolically, the iconostasis represents a religious presence during services, a filter through which the faithful may worship. Orthodox believers always pray standing, light candles as offerings, and often kiss the icons as a sign of respect and supplication. The combined experience is intended to convey the mysterious essence of the faith. The priest will wear garments that have a symbolic meaning according to the ceremony.

The Church of Cyprus is estimated to have more than 600,000 members, divided among six diocese across the island.

71

THE MONASTIC LIFE

Monasticism is a long established and essential feature of the Orthodox tradition, growing out the Roman emperor Constantine's unification of state and church. Cypriots are proud of their monastic traditions and institutions, especially the magnificent hilltop monasteries of Panagia tou Kykkou, Machairas, and Stavrovouni. The monasteries have borne the ideals of Orthodox Christendom through time in the face of numerous foreign invasions and occupations. Cyprus contributes more monks to the monastic enclave of Mount Athos, the most important center of Orthodoxy in northern Greece, than any other Orthodox country.

Although numbers are falling, people still join monasteries. The Stavrovouni Monastery, near Larnaca, is considered the strictest on the island. It is where 20 or so monks maintain the traditional monastic lifestyle. Most of the monks are young and have to be highly committed to a life that makes great demands on them. Their day is divided equally between prayer and study, physical labor, and rest. During the rest periods, the monks eat two frugal meals without meat and carry out nightly prayers that constantly interrupt their sleep. The main liturgies (prayers) of the day are practiced in the courtyard. They include predawn "matins," the main liturgy after sunrise, "vespers" before the evening meal, and "compline" later in the evening. Winters in the monastery are very severe, making the monks' farming activities difficult. The monks still paint icons, which are of a very high standard, while many monasteries produce their own wine and make their own jam and honey.

Other monasteries, such as Ayios Neophytos near Paphos, are popular places of pilgrimage. Ayios Neophytos was established by Neophytos, a local saint, in the 12th century. Neophytos, who had come to the hills of Paphos to seek solitude, cut a hermitage into the rocks with his own hands. Soon, a sizeable community sprang up around the famous monk, who was revered for his holiness and wisdom. He was a scholar of considerable note, and his handbook on monastic life, *Ritual Ordinance*, survives to this day. Today, pilgrims come to see the bones of the monk in the cave hermitage and to view the beautiful religious frescoes painted by followers of Neophytos.

ISLAM

Opposite: **Turkish Cypriots picnic outside the Hala Sultan Mosque to mark the end of the holy month of Ramadan.**

Cyprus's Turkish minority are almost exclusively Sunni Muslims. Authority for the Muslim religion in Cyprus is the mufti, an expert in Islamic law, and the *Koran* ("KOH-rahn"), the Muslim holy book. Generally, the Muslims in Cyprus are not as devout as their mainland counterparts. Islam has never been politically or socially dominant on the island. This can partly be explained by the mixed background of the island's Muslim community, who had in the past intermarried with both Lusignan and Venetian Christians. In the Ottoman period, a sect, called Linovamvaki, practiced Islam outwardly but maintained Christian beliefs in private.

Other sects included the 13th century Mevlevi Order, which stressed music and dance as a way of expressing love of God. It lasted until 1954. The Ba'hai sect from Iran has also had substantial support in recent years. Given these unconventional influences, it is not surprising that Turkish Cypriots are not particularly orthodox Muslims. The more obvious expressions of Islamic devotion, such as wearing religious dress and growing long beards, are not popular with Turkish Cypriots. Islamic law, or *shari'ah* ("SHAR-i-ah"), is not practiced in north Cyprus or Turkey.

Islamic principles differ slightly from those of Christians. Although Muslims believe the Bible is a sacred book and recognize the teaching of the biblical prophets, they do not accept the divinity of Jesus because he is merely a prophet. Muslims consider Mohammed the greatest and final prophet, the carrier of God's message to mankind. However, they do not worship Mohammed, only God, and God's revelations to Mohammed are contained in the *Koran*. Before beginning prayer, Muslims first wash their hands, arms, feet, ankles, head, and neck in running water. If water is not available, the ritual motions will suffice. They must then cover their head, face Mecca, and perform a precise series of genuflections.

ISLAMIC SECTS

A number of high-profile Islamic sects have prospered in north Cyprus recently. The best known is led by the charismatic Kibrisli Seyh Nazim, who leads the Naqshbandi order of Sufism. The headquarters of his organization—the Turkish Cypriot Islamic Society—is in Lefke, near Morphou Bay. There are also groups abroad, including London. The society campaigns for greater piety in the lax religious atmosphere of the north and stresses the authority of the spiritual leader.

Currently, the sect numbers less than a thousand. Some well-known local and international figures have at different times been followers of Kibrisli Seyh Nazim. Rauf Denktash, the TRNC president, is a former adherent, and the American singer Cat Stevens and the British rock musician Bob Geldof are more recent supporters.

OTHER FAITHS

Maronite Christians come from Lebanon, where the Maronite church is one of the largest eastern branches of the Roman Catholic Church. There are about 10,000 Maronite worshippers in Cyprus today. Most of them live in the south of Cyprus and have in part assimilated into the Greek Cypriot community. The church traces its origins to Saint Maron, a fourth century Syrian hermit. The immediate spiritual leader of the Maronite church, after the Pope, is the patriarch of Antioch, who resides in Bkirki, near Beirut. The patriarch of Antioch remains head of the Catholic churches in the Middle East. Despite papal attempts to Latinize their rites, the church retains the ancient West Syrian liturgy, although the vernacular language of the Maronites is Arabic. For some years, the Maronites have celebrated Easter at the same time as the island's Orthodox community, in part because it is convenient.

There are also a few thousand practicing Roman Catholics in Cyprus. Catholicism has a long history on the island. Under Lusignan rule, Catholicism was the religion of the local aristocracy. Many of the island's great religious buildings date from this time. They include the St. Sophia cathedral in Nicosia, the St. Nicholas cathedral in Famagusta, and the

Abbey of Bellapais near Kyrenia. All of these buildings have since been converted to mosques or Orthodox institutions.

There are a little over 3,000 Armenians in Cyprus who practice the Armenian Apostolic faith. The Armenian Apostolic Church was founded in the late third century by Gregory the Illuminator. In converting the Armenian king, Gregory in effect created the world's first truly Christian state. The Armenian Church separated from the other Eastern churches in the sixth century and is completely autonomous. It is headed by the Catholicos of Echmiadzin, near Yerevan, in Armenia.

Anglicans in Cyprus also number a few thousand. They are sustained by the island's small British population.

The Abbey of Bellapais is about 800 years old.

LANGUAGE

IN THE ORIGINAL CONSTITUTION of the Republic of Cyprus, both Greek and Turkish are recognized as official languages of the island. In reality, Greek has become the official language of the Republic of Cyprus, while in the north, the official language is Turkish. Both the Greek and Turkish spoken on Cyprus are distinct dialects and differ from the languages of Greece and Turkey. It is estimated that about 15% of the words in the two local languages are peculiar to Cyprus. Curiously, to the untrained ear, Cypriot Greek and Turkish sound almost identical because of the strong intonation and accent. In the republic, English is also widely spoken. This is partly a result of the British colonial past, but mainly because of the longtime presence of British military bases and the huge numbers of English-speaking tourists who visit the island each year. Speaking English is still seen as a badge of sophistication and education among Cypriots, both Greeks and Turks.

Opposite: **Many signs use English and either Turkish or Greek to cater to the growing number of English-speaking tourists flocking to the country.**

Left: **Many older Cypriots are able to speak English because they grew up under a British administration. Since independence, the language has become a compulsory subject in school.**

GREEK

Greek is an Indo-European language that can be traced back to the 14th century B.C., making it one of the oldest languages in the world. Many of the writing systems used today are based on ancient Greek. In ancient times, Greek was widely spoken throughout the eastern Mediterranean.

While the majority of the Greek Cypriot population speak Greek, a local dialect has developed over many centuries. To some mainlanders, the dialect seems to be a completely different language. Certain sounds in standard Greek are almost completely absent from Cypriot Greek, while in some regional dialects, such as in Paphos, the spoken language has been heavily influenced by Turkish words.

Greek is not an easy language to learn. The positioning of stress is an important part of speaking Greek, and emphasizing the correct syllable is essential for clear communication. An incorrect stress will render words unintelligible, or possibly change their meaning altogether. For example, the word *yéros* ("YEH-ros"), with a stress on the "e," means "old man,"

THE GREEK ALPHABET

The Greek alphabet used today was formed as far back as the Hellenistic period (300–100 B.C.), and has heavily influenced the formation of other alphabets, including the Roman alphabet. There are 24 letters in the Greek alphabet, and 13 main combinations or diphthongs.

Α,α	a	"a" as father		Ο,ο	o	"o" as in toad
Β,β	v	"v" as in vet		Π,π	p	"p" as in put
Γ,γ	y	"y" as in yes				(sometimes like a "b" sound)
Δ,δ	dh	"the" as in then		Ρ,ρ	r	"r" as in terror
Ε,ε	e	"e" as in wet		Σ,σ	s	"s" as in sat
Ζ,ζ	z	"z" as in zebra		Τ,τ	t	"t" as in tight
Η,η	i	"i" as in ski				(sometimes like a "d" sound)
Θ,θ	th	"th" as in theme		Υ,υ	i or y	"i" as in ski
Ι,ι	i	"i" as in ski		Φ,φ	f	"f" as in fish
Κ,κ	k	"g" as in get		Χ,χ	kh	"ch" as in loch
Λ,λ	l	"l" as in lolly		Ψ,ψ	ps	"ps" as in lips
Μ,μ	m	"m" as in man		Ω,ω	o	"o" as in toad
Ν,ν	n	"n" as in no				
Ξ,ξ	ks	combination of "k" and "s," not found in English				

while the same sounds with a stress on the "o," as in *yerós* ("yeh-ROS"), means "sturdy." Greek has a number of longer vowel sounds, where two vowels appear side by side. The two vowels are usually read together as a single sound. However, if an accent is placed above the first vowel, the two sounds are pronounced separately, and the first vowel sound is given emphasis. Despite these difficulties, Greek is a very beautiful spoken language.

In conversation, Greek speakers differentiate between informal and formal address, and young people, older people, and rural folk almost always use informal forms, even with strangers. There are numerous words and phrases that are constantly used in Greek. The most common greeting is *yá sou* ("YA soo"), meaning "health to you," while *ti néa* ("tee NEH-ah"), meaning "what's new," is also used. If a Greek Cypriot wishes to express dismay, he or she will say *pó-pó-pó* ("POH-poh-poh"). *Ópa* ("OH-pah") means "watch it" or "whoops," and if Greek speakers want you to slow down and relax, they will say *sigá sigá* ("see-GAH see-GAH").

The Greek Cypriot dialect is said to have undeniable Homeric origins, supporting the widely-held belief that the island's Greek inhabitants are descendants of Mycenean Greeks from the Trojan Wars.

A Turkish-speaking fruit and vegetable vendor in Paphos.

TURKISH

The Turkish language is a member of the Turkic family of languages, spoken by more than 150 million people living from the borders of China to the Balkans in southeast Europe. Modern Turkish is a descendant of Ottoman Turkish, which itself descends from Old Anatolian. Turkish has over the centuries absorbed a great many Persian and Arabic words.

The Cypriot Turkish dialect is quite distinct from standard Turkish on the mainland. Turkish Cypriot usage is also very casual. Turks from Istanbul, for example, consider Cypriot Turkish a slovenly dialect, while the Turkish Cypriots view standard Turkish politeness and formality with amusement. Regional dialects also exist. Paphiot Turkish, spoken by Turkish Cypriot refugees from the Paphos district, shows the effects of a long cohabitation with Greek, containing many Greek words or variations of Greek words. However, the influx of mainland Turks and two decades of Turkish army occupation means mainland Turkish is becoming increasingly influential. Some peculiarities of the dialect are steadily being eroded. The influence of Turkish television has also contributed to the harmonizing of the two languages. Sadly, the Cypriot Turkish dialect could disappear over the next two generations, as the north slowly becomes absorbed by the mainland.

Turkish is notoriously difficult to learn for speakers of Western European languages, as the grammatical structure is unrelated to any Romance or Indo-European languages, and the word order is difficult.

THE TURKISH ALPHABET

Until 1928, Turkish was written in the Arabic alphabet. Since it was deemed unsuitable for representing the sounds of Turkish, the language underwent radical reforms with Arabic letters being replaced by the Latin alphabet. Today, the Turkish alphabet has 29 letters—eight vowels and 21 consonants.

a	"a" as in m<u>a</u>n		m	"m" as in <u>m</u>ud
b	"b" as in <u>b</u>et		n	"n" as in <u>n</u>ot
c	"j" as in jam		o	"o" as in h<u>o</u>t
ç	"ch" as in <u>ch</u>urch		ö	"er" as in oth<u>er</u>
d	"d" as in <u>d</u>ad		p	"p" as in <u>p</u>ot
e	"e" as in b<u>e</u>d		r	"r" as in <u>r</u>ibbon
f	"f" as in <u>f</u>at		s	"s" as in <u>s</u>ing
g	"g" as in <u>g</u>oat		ş	"sh" as <u>sh</u>all
ğ	"y" as in <u>y</u>et		t	"t" as in <u>t</u>ake
h	"h" as in <u>h</u>ouse		u	"u" as in p<u>u</u>sh
ı	"i" as in cous<u>i</u>n		ü	"ew" as in y<u>ew</u>
i	"i" as in p<u>i</u>t		v	"v" as in <u>v</u>ast
j	"s" as in trea<u>s</u>ure		y	"y" as in <u>y</u>et
k	"k" as in <u>k</u>ey		z	"z" as in <u>z</u>ebra
l	"l" as in <u>l</u>and			

Turkish is characterized by a tendency to expand from an unchanging root word to which one or more of a vast array of suffixes or word endings are attached to alter meaning. For example: *bilgi* ("bihl-GEE") means "knowledge," while *bilgisiz* ("bihl-gee-SIHZ") means "without knowledge," and *bilgisizlik* ("bihl-gee-sihz-LIHK") becomes "lack of knowledge."

However, Turkish pronunciation is easier than Greek because the spelling is phonetic, and words are pronounced as they are spelled. Turkish vowels are usually short, and unlike Greek, there are no dipthongs, or vowel combinations—each vowel retains its individual sound. Stress is generally placed on the last syllable of a word, with the exception of place names. Typical Turkish greetings include *"Nasilsiniz"* ("nah-sihl-sih-NIHZ") and *"Ne haber"* ("neh hah-BER"), both meaning "How are you," while typical phrases include *"bir dakika"* ("bih dah-kih-KAH"), or "wait a minute," and *"affedersiniz"* ("ahf-ehd-ehr-sih-NIHZ"), meaning "sorry" or "I beg your pardon."

Newspapers on sale at a newsstand.

NEWSPAPERS

Cypriots are a highly literate, news-hungry people, as reflected in the large number of newspapers and periodicals published on the island. This is partly a product of political organizations, such as trade unions and political parties, sponsoring publications on both sides of the divide. In the republic, popular daily papers in Greek include *Alithia* (Truth), a right-wing organ that supports the DISY party, and the moderate papers *Apogevmatini* (Afternoon) and *O Phileleftheros* (The Liberal). *Ergatiki Phoni* (Workers' Voice), a popular weekly trade union paper established since 1947, has a circulation of 10,000. *Ergatiko Vima* (Workers' Tribune), is another union organ with a circulation of 14,000. Periodicals include the widely-read *To Periodico* (The Periodical), established in 1986, and *I Kypria* (The Cypriot Woman), a bimonthly women's magazine.

Popular English language papers include the daily *Cyprus Mail*, which has a circulation of 4,000, and the popular weekly paper *Cyprus Weekly*, with a circulation of 12,000. While the latter has become increasingly anti-Turkish, both are renowned for their news coverage. *The Blue Beret* is a monthly English-language publication for the UN forces posted in Cyprus.

In the Turkish North, *Kibris* (Cyprus) is the bestselling right-wing daily newspaper in the Turkish language, with a circulation of 13,000. Other popular dailies include *Birlik* (Unity) and *Halkin Sesi* (People's Voice). *Cyprus Today*, owned by the Turkish Cypriot businessman Asil Nadir (who also owns *Kibris*), is the north's only English-language publication.

RADIO AND TELEVISION

The Cyprus Broadcasting Corporation (CyBC) began operations in 1957. Its three radio channels broadcast programs in Greek, English, Turkish, and Armenian. An international service also broadcasts in English and Arabic. More than 20 smaller radio stations operate across the island. The CyBC runs three television stations, broadcasting in Greek and Turkish. It also imports many English programs. Greek programs from the mainland can be received via satellite, as can international satellite channels such as CNN and Star TV. The British Services Broadcasting Service from the British military base at Akrotiri can be received throughout the island.

In north Cyprus, the state-run Bayrak Radio (and) Television Corporation (BRT) broadcasts radio programs mainly in Turkish and some programs in Greek, English, German, and Arabic from their station in Nicosia. Bayrak TV also shows television programs in Turkish, Greek, Arabic, and English across nine channels. In addition, two mainland Turkish television channels broadcast in Turkish to north Cyprus.

A British military radar station on Mount Olympus, for monitoring the airwaves in the region. With ethnic and cross-border tensions occasionally surfacing, both CyBC and BRT are sometimes guilty of using their broadcasts for propaganda purposes. Bayrak radio will often broadcast Greek music to attract Greek listeners as a prelude to news programs that cast the south in a bad light. Similarly, CyBC in its Turkish-language programs, will always refer to the north as "Turkish-occupied territory."

ARTS

IN ITS LONG AND TURBULENT HISTORY, Cyprus has played host to many different visitors. The impact of the Greek, Roman, Persian, Byzantine, and Ottoman civilizations and the Crusaders is evident in the architecture and artistic remains on the island.

Traditional music and dance are the most important and most popular arts in Cyprus. They have changed little over the centuries because of the isolation of a predominantly rural population. On both sides of the border, the governments have made considerable efforts to protect the medieval and ancient heritage of the island. In the north, the Department of Antiquities has carried out restoration work. In the south, archaeological digs and restoration projects have been able to attract international aid, especially when linked to the development of tourism. For this reason, Paphos, Curium, and Amathus are well-excavated sites, while sites such as Soli in the north still require extensive work.

Opposite: **A fine example of the intricately-woven cloths by Cypriots.**

Left: **The ancient amphi-theater at Curium. After being restored, it is now sometimes used to stage ancient Greek and modern dramas.**

ANCIENT HERITAGE

Cyprus is home to a vast ancient heritage that has been unearthed in archaeological digs over the years. Many of the best finds are in the island's various museums, including district museums in Larnaca, Limassol, and Paphos, the Pieredes Foundation Museum in Larnaca, and the Cyprus Museum in southern Nicosia. Unfortunately, only a small portion of Cyprus's ancient heritage has remained on the island. Many art objects were removed by European archaeologists in the 19th and early 20th centuries, and now found in museums all over the world.

Many figurines, some of extremely high quality, have survived from the Chalcolithic or copperstone period (3800–2800 B.C.). The figures, usually made from picrolite, a soft, blue-green stone, include outstanding anthropomorphic cruciforms, idols, and female fertility symbols. Copper items from the Bronze Age (2300–1050 B.C.) confirm the island's reputation for metal work. Many bronze items, especially jewelry and vessels, were discovered in the royal tombs at Salamis. Many beautiful handmade vases survive from this time. Terracotta figures, including toys and female fertility figures, date from the Archaic period (750–475 B.C.). This period was also remarkable for its beautiful, embossed gold plaques and jewelry.

The Classical period produced some large sculpture. The figures wore Greek dress and had beards, reflecting the influence of Persia. The figures include an impressive representation of Aphrodite of Soli, which has become a popular symbol of Cyprus. Hellenistic art shows Athenian and Alexandrian influences, especially in the statues of local rulers and officials. The gold and jewelry of this period is magnificent. The Roman period is most famous for mosaics. Excellent examples at Soli depict a waterfowl flanked by dolphins, and a swan enclosed by floral patterns. At Salamis, there are mosaics of the river god, Evrotas, and partial remnants of a battle scene. At Curium, fifth century mosaics depict scenes from the Trojan War and Greek mythology, while others have animals and geometric shapes indicating growing Christian influences.

Ancient architecture includes the impressive sites of Curium, with its Roman-built temple of Apollo Hylates, and the temple of Aphrodite at Amathus. The most impressive ancient remains are at Salamis, north of Famagusta. Most of the ruins at Salamis date from the Hellenistic, Roman, and Byzantine periods. They include a gymnasium, baths, amphitheater, and 150 royal tombs from the seventh and eighth centuries B.C.

A mosaic in the House of Aion, one of the four ancient sites in Paphos. This mosaic is part of a collection of mosaics discovered in a cluster of buildings from the Roman period.

Like the Selimiye mosque in Nicosia, the Lala Mustapha Pasha mosque *(above)* in Famagusta was originally a church, the St. Nicholas cathedral. The Lusignans built it in the early 14th century. Although a minaret has been incongruously positioned on top of one of its towers, St. Nicholas's Gothic grace makes it one of the most beautiful buildings in Cyprus.

MEDIEVAL ARCHITECTURE

Lusignan rule left a considerable architectural legacy in Cyprus, introducing fine, Gothic architecture to the island at a time when western Europe was achieving its architectural zenith. One of these buildings is the Selimiye Mosque, a former cathedral, in the heart of old Nicosia. Originally built as St. Sophia cathedral by French architects in 1209, its broad outline resembles some of the magnificent medieval cathedrals of France. Following the Ottoman occupation, in 1571 the cathedral was converted to a mosque and all Christian decorations removed.

Famagusta is home to some of the most impressive medieval architecture in the Middle East. The famous painter Leonardo da Vinci is said to have been involved in the construction of the Venetian-style fortifications. The walls of Famagusta have a squat appearance—in some places they are 49 feet (15 m) tall and 26 feet (8 m) thick.

Cyprus has numerous examples of Renaissance military architecture. Some of the most elaborate include the castles at Kyrenia, St. Hilarion,

Buffavento, and Kantara. These are all situated in the Kyrenia Mountains. St. Hilarion castle, for example, was built originally by the Byzantines, mainly as a defense against Arab raiders and pirates. Nicosia's city walls contain a fascinating mixture of architecture that reflects the city's turbulent history. The walls were originally built by the Venetians in the 16th century. Though not high, they are extremely thick and were designed to allow cannon to be rolled along the ramparts.

Cyprus has many magnificent, isolated monasteries in the mountains. The ruins of Sourp Magar monastery nestles amid the Kyrenia Mountains. Like many of the island's monasteries, it is a vestige of the Cypriot church's powerful and wealthy past. Antiphonitis monastery, which contains many exquisite frescoes, is one of the most architecturally impressive religious buildings in Cyprus. Other well-known monasteries include the Stavrovouni monastery, perched on a rocky crag to the west of Larnaca. The monastery has a long and illustrious history. Founded by St. Helena in A.D. 327, the monastery is thought to have contained a fragment of the Biblical True Cross. The monastery was burned in both Lusignan times and by the Ottomans. The present building dates from the 19th century.

A medieval castle in bright stone, the Kolossi castle is surrounded by orchards.

The Kykko monastery in the Troodos Mountains and the monastery of Ayios Chrysostomos on the southern slopes of the Kyrenia range were built in the 11th century. They are classic examples of late Byzantine monastic architecture. The 13th century Abbey at Bellapais near Kyrenia boasts an impressive cloister, church, and magnificent refectory.

ICON PAINTING

A long-standing bastion of the Orthodox Christian religion, beautiful icons
and frescos have been painted in the churches and monasteries of Cyprus
since Byzantine times. Icons are the principal religious art form of the
Orthodox faith, transmitting to the faithful the glory of God. Depictions of
Biblical scenes and scenes from liturgical history, and images of the Virgin
Mary, Jesus, and the Apostles offer physical representations to inspire and
direct the faith of worshippers. Icons are not merely works of art, but are
imbued with religious significance and venerated by the faithful. Literally
hundreds of churches all over the island are intricately decorated with
religious reliefs and icons.

Icon painting began in the early Byzantine period, in the sixth century.
Cyprus became a refuge for icon painters during the eighth and ninth
centuries, when there were doctrinal disputes over whether it was
appropriate to worship images. Because of this theological controversy,
icons were destroyed in great numbers. Many of the more impressive

church paintings found today are derived from the later Byzantine period, in the 10th–12th centuries. Many have faded beyond recognition, but some remarkable ones can be found at Ayios Trypiotis in Nicosia, Ayios Lazaros in Larnaca, the Apostolos Andreas monastery on the Karpas Peninsula. Some of the best icon painters in Europe practiced their art on the island, including the 14th century master Philip Goul, who decorated the churches of Stavros tou Ayiasmati and Ayios Mamas at Louvaras, located high in the Troodos Mountains. Typical paintings depict scenes from the Bible, illustrating the lives of Jesus and the Apostles. In the chapel of Ayios Mamas, impressive frescoes depict Jesus healing the sick and blind, the Last Supper, and John the Baptist. Recently, icons were collected together in the Byzantine Museum in Nicosia and the Icon Museum in Kyrenia.

Icon painting is highly stylized. The subject is captured with a perfect visage, frozen for eternity. Naturalistic representations are rare. Today, icon-making continues in the monasteries, expressing religious fervor and devotion.

ART THIEVES

A Byzantine mosaic depicting the Virgin, the baby Jesus, and the Apostles, estimated to be from the fifth or sixth century (possibly the oldest fresco on the island), was stolen by black-market dealers from the Kanakaria church on the Karpas Peninsula. A little-visited church, it was not noticed until 1979 that some enterprising thieves had broken in and hacked off sections of the mosaic from the wall, spiriting them off the island. The whereabouts of the mosaics were not discovered until the late 1980s, when an art dealer in the United States paid more than a million dollars for them to a Swiss intermediary. They were subsequently offered for sale to the Getty Museum in California for 10 times the amount. However, the Church of Cyprus and government soon found out about the deal and sued for the return of the treasure. They eventually won their case, and the mosaics were returned to Cyprus in 1991. Today, they are displayed in the Archbishop Makarios Cultural Center in southern Nicosia.

The Turkish victory monument in Famagusta is one of the many sculptures in Cyprus commemorating the people who have perished in the clashes between Greeks and Turks over the years.

MODERN PAINTING AND SCULPTURE

Modern art did not develop in Cyprus until the beginning of the 20th century, following trends in Europe. Since then, Cypriot artists have sought to capture the moods and nuances of the landscape. One of Cyprus's better known painters and sculptors, Christoforos Savva (1924–1968), painted in an innovative post-Cubist style using sharp, magnificent colors. His most famous works are *Nude* (1957), and the abstract *Composition with Two Circles* (1967). Other leading Cypriot artists include Stass Paraskos, born in 1933, who is influenced by the island's artistic and archaeological heritage, the Constructivist Stelios Votsis, who was born in 1929, and the Expressionist Vera Hadjida, born in 1936. Andreas Savvides, born in 1930, has produced work that includes monumental sculpture and abstract compositions combining different materials.

LITERATURE

Modern Cypriot literature is not well established or widely read outside the island. One reason is that the Greek Cypriot dialect is different from the mainland language, making widespread distribution of Greek Cypriot writing very difficult. Among writers on both sides of the divide, poetry is the most popular medium of expression. Political-literary magazines, such as the left-wing *Nea Epochi* (New Epoch) and the literary monthly *Pnevmatiki Kypros* (Intellectual Cyprus), indicate the vibrancy of Greek Cypriots' interest in modern literature.

HANDICRAFTS

Folk art is still alive and well in Cyprus, and weaving and lacework are still a part of the lives of many Cypriot women, especially in the villages. It has been argued that Cypriot arts and crafts have their origin in the need of young women to be provided with a dowry. Men would craft objects of copper, gourds, and wood. Mothers and daughters would also produce great quantities of embroidered linen for the bride's dowry, to provide bedsheets, pillow cases, furniture coverings, towels, and floor covers. Today, the picturesque village of Lefkara, in the foothills of the Troodos Mountains west of Larnaca, is the center of this craft tradition, famous for its lace embroidery and silver creations.

While Lefkara's lace industry prospers, the same cannot be said of other cottage industries in Cyprus. High-quality pottery and ceramics, for example, have been produced in Cyprus for many centuries, but producers have found themselves unable to compete internationally. In the past, *pitharia* ("PIH-thah-ree-ah"), containers three feet (about one meter) in diameter and made by highly-regarded craftsmen, were produced for storing olive oil, olives, and wine. Today, they are often used to hold flowers in gardens. Small pottery, including glazed vases, figurines, bowls, and pitchers, is the specialty of the Paphos district. These are often decorated with floral patterns or geometric designs reminiscent of their ancient counterparts. Gourd flasks have also been made for centuries, though they are little used today. Wickerwork and basketry are also a common sight.

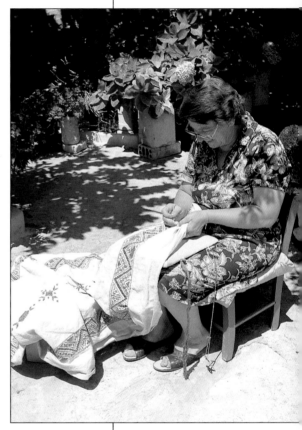

A woman making lace in Lefkara. This village is a popular place for tourists who come from afar to buy embroidered lace.

DANCE AND SONG

In Cyprus, music and dance are traditionally the most popular art forms. Today, traditional forms are threatened by disco and pop music, especially Greek pop music, which is increasingly played on many festive occasions. Most Cypriot boys and girls learn to dance both traditional and modern variations of traditional dances at school. Some purists believe that while dance classes in school are useful to ensure a wide knowledge of Cypriot dance, the classes also limit the spontaneity of the performers by encouraging uniformity of movement.

Dances are usually performed on special occasions, such as at weddings, or on festival days. In the past, men would dance not only on festive occasions, but also in coffeehouses in the evening, or even on the threshing floor. Today, the occasions for dancing are more restricted. Cypriot dances are of many kinds, most of which can be performed by both men and women. Traditionally, men danced with men, and women with women. The only exception was when the bride danced with the groom at a wedding party. More recently, mixed dancing has been introduced, although traditionalists frown on such developments.

Greek Cypriot men dancing to the rhythm of a folk song during a festive celebration.

Stylistically, men's dances are usually more lively, women's dances more delicate and restrained. The best-known dance is the *kartchilamas* ("gar-chee-LAH-mahs"), performed by pairs of male and female dancers. Often, this will form the foundation for a much broader suite, rounded off with more complicated dances such as the *syrtos* ("SEE-tohs"), and *mandra* ("MAHN-drah"). The *syrtos* is a particularly popular dance at social gatherings, such as weddings. The *kartchilamas*, a very lively dance, offers the men the opportunity to compete with each other and demonstrate their strength, while the women's dances tend to stress restraint and grace. Stamping feet on one spot is a typical feature of the *kartchilamas* and the *syrtos*. The *dhrepanin* ("threh-PAH-neen"), or "sickle dance," has an agricultural theme, where the male dancers cut imaginary swathes in the air and around their bodies as they mow the harvest. This dance is particularly popular at the festival *Kataklismós*, and allows male dancers to express themselves energetically. In the women's dances, the woman stays in one spot, and much of the movement is in the positioning of the arms and the turning of the body.

Cypriots take great pride in their traditional folk songs. Love songs, working songs, children's rhymes, humorous songs, wedding songs, laments, and political rhymes are all part of the Cypriot cannon. The most popular rhythm is the *kalamatianos* ("gar-LAH-mah-tee-ah-nohs"), a tempo with ancient origins.

In its purest and most traditional form, music is played on a shepherd's flute, or *auloi* ("ow-LOH-ee"). The violin and flute are used to accompany dance performances. Another traditional instrument is the *laoudo* ("LAH-oo-doh")*,* or long-necked flute. Turkish traditional instruments include the *zorna* ("zoh-NAH"), a kind of oboe, the *davul* ("dah-VUHL"), a two-headed drum, and the *kasat* ("kah-SAHT"), or small finger cymbals. But with a rising appetite for modern pop music, traditional music and instruments are in decline.

A medieval-style musician playing outside a castle wall.

LEISURE

AS A POPULAR HOLIDAY DESTINATION, modern Cyprus is, in the minds of many people, associated with leisure. This is an image that the casual Cypriots are happy to cultivate. Sitting, drinking, and eating with friends, whether in a taverna, restaurant, or coffeeshop, remain the most popular and traditional ways to relax for most Cypriots. Backgammon, an ancient game played in this part of the world, is the most common indoor game. It is played by men almost everywhere on the island.

The island's warm and dry climate, rugged landscape, and varied coastline have resulted in Cyprus gaining a reputation as an outdoor sports paradise. It is also an excellent place to engage in water sports. Other activities such as mountain biking, cycling, and hiking, have become extremely popular with visitors to Cyprus. Golf is also heavily promoted. Traditional sports, such as soccer and hunting, remain predominant among the local people.

Opposite: **Many fishing enthusiasts are more interested in enjoying the tranquil, picturesque coastal view than getting a bountiful catch.**

Left: **These two Cypriot men, engaged in a serious game of backgammon, are concentrating hard on making the next move.**

97

RURAL PURSUITS

Cyprus's warm climate makes it an ideal location for outdoor activities. Family picnics on Sundays or festival days are popular. The whole family will travel to the coast or the countryside and eat kebabs in the shade of an olive tree. The low temperatures in the Troodos Mountains make the area an ideal place to relax.

Nature trails have been recently marked along the coast and in the mountains. Hikers, often tourists, can easily follow signs that give details of the local flora and fauna in Greek and English.

Cyprus boasts of one leisure activity that is considered exotic in the Middle East—skiing. There is a ski resort on the northeast face of Mount Olympus in the Troodos Mountains. It is opened from January to early April. An international ski event, which attracts top skiers from around the world, is held in February.

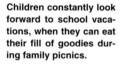

Children constantly look forward to school vacations, when they can eat their fill of goodies during family picnics.

HUNTING

The hunting of small game and birds has traditionally been popular in Cyprus. In the 1970s it was estimated that as many as 10 million birds were killed each year in Cyprus—more than 15 birds for every man, woman, and child on the island! While this number has since decreased, and some species have become protected in nature reserves, the activity remains popular. The hills around the village of Dipkarpas on the Karpas Peninsula are considered the best spot on the island for hunting of birds. In the hunting season, which lasts from November to January, the road is thick with vehicles and men in camouflage jackets, seeking partridge and francolin. The sport is so popular that men travel from Morphou, which is at the other end of the island, to participate. The catch is normally taken home and cooked. Hares and rabbits are also hunted.

Horse-riding in the sun-baked Akamas Peninsula is a popular pastime for both tourists and Cypriots.

BEACH LIFE

For a destination promoted as a holiday paradise, Cyprus has only a few pleasant beaches. In the north, however, there are some outstanding, secluded coves and bays for swimming. The stretch of Famagusta Bay, for example, is considered one of the finest beaches in the Mediterranean. There are also many small beaches along the northern coast to the west and east of Kyrenia. The most popular beaches are at Lara Bay and Alakati. The former is famous as a breeding ground for loggerhead turtles and a vital environmental resource—during the breeding season, the beach is reserved for turtles. Other beaches along the northern coast are used by the North Cypriots, and on the weekends they become crowded with

The beautiful Coral Bay beach, situated several miles north of Paphos, is packed with vacationers. The beach has one of the longest and finest stretches of golden sand in the area.

families having barbecues and enjoying the sea air. The southern coastline of the Karpas Peninsula has some of the island's most beautiful, inaccessible, and unspoiled beaches. Here, the Nangomí beach, which runs for three miles (4.8 km), is probably the best—and cleanest—beach on the entire island, with not a soft drink bottle or taverna in sight.

Many of the tourist beaches in the south have been artificially created, especially around Limassol and Paphos, where the shore has improved with sand brought from elsewhere. Other good beaches include Governor's beach, 20 miles (32 km) east of Limassol, and Pissouri beach, west of the British base at Episkopi. While the beaches around Ayia Napa provide some good stretches of sand, every inch is filled by the many thousands of tourists who visit this area. Although the beaches in the south are of a poorer quality, they tend to have more facilities, with water sports, beach-side tavernas, drink vendors, beach furniture, and children's playgrounds all provided. Throughout the south, it is difficult to find the seclusion that defines the north. The exception is the isolated and often off-limits Akamas Peninsula, where a number of excellent unspoiled beaches remain, protected by British military rights to practice bombing and firing.

The island's huge tourist industry has led to an explosion of water and beach sports, including windsurfing, water-skiing, speedboating, dinghy sailing, jet-skiing, scuba diving, and parasailing. Some beaches even have bungee-jumping facilities. These activities are based around the hotels and are most popular with tourists and expatriates. The capes near Paphos, Ayia Napa, and Protaris are the most popular spots for windsurfing, while sailing is popular in the bays off Larnaca and Limassol. Diving is popular in waters all around the island, thanks to the crystal clear water and rocky coastline. Submarine cliffs and valleys, coral, and exotic sea life provide plenty of underwater attractions for divers.

The best beach used to be at Glossa, to the south of Varosha. Now, it is deserted, a result of the evacuation of Varosha in 1974.

Like many aspects of island life, soccer has become a symbol of the divisions and differences. Cyprus has had two separate soccer federations since 1955. The Republic of Cyprus refuses to recognize any teams from the North, and vice-versa.

CITY FUN

Traditionally, Cypriots of all ages spend their time chatting over food and drinks for the whole evening in their favorite taverna or restaurant. While Cypriots tend to avoid the resort areas such as Ayia Napa, many young Cypriots enjoy the night life of Nicosia, Limassol, and Paphos. The rapid expansion of the island's tourist scene has led to an explosion of clubs, bars, and restaurants in the main tourist areas. Night clubs, bars, and pubs have only been recently introduced to Cyprus. They tend to be patronized by the young and more liberal-minded Cypriots.

Movies are also popular in Cyprus, especially international and American ones. These films usually have Greek or Turkish subtitles, depending on which side of the border they are shown. Big movie-houses pack in moviegoers in Nicosia, Larnaca, and Limassol.

BATHS

Turkish baths can be found in many parts of the Middle East and Eastern Mediterranean, and in many of the cities of Cyprus. One of the largest and best-known, the Büyük Hammam, which means the Grand Baths, lies in northern Nicosia. It provides traditional Turkish baths. Fridays are reserved for women, but all other days are for men only. The treatment includes an exposure to warm air, then steam, followed by a massage, and finally a cold shower. Most baths have separate washrooms and soaking pools.

Bathers spend many happy hours sweating in the hot rooms, followed by washing with a camel hair glove, or perhaps a vigorous massage by a masseur. The bath is considered an excellent way to lose weight, cleanse the skin, and generally relax the mind and body. Those who believe in the medicinal qualities of the Turkish bath try to visit as often as possible—at least once a month, or even once a week.

SPORTS

Soccer remains the most popular sport on the island, both north and south of the divide, and attracts more spectators than any other sport. While Cyprus has made little impact in European club or international competitions, the sport is followed with great enthusiasm, and leading teams such as Omonia Nicosia draw wide support. Cypriots also like tennis, both as players and spectators, and courts in the hotels and public areas of the towns in the south are always booked.

Although Cyprus is not in the forefront of world athletics, the island has strong athletic traditions, stretching back to the time of the ancient Greeks. Cypriots are also thought to have participated in the earliest Olympic games. With the Ottoman occupation and arrival of the Turks, weightlifting was encouraged as the national sport.

Every September, the Cyprus Car Rally attracts entries from many world-class championship drivers. The winding tracks and rugged landscape offer competitors a tough test of their driving abilities.

The love for soccer has been passed from one generation to the next. From an early age, Cypriot boys will learn to play soccer.

FESTIVALS

IN THE GREEK SOUTH, public holidays and festivals tend to have a religious focus, reflecting the dominant position of the Orthodox Church in Greek Cypriot culture. Recently, tourist authorities have organized many special events to attract foreigners. In the north, which is a secular society, people celebrate significant events in Turkish Cypriot communal history and a few imported festivals from the mainland.

While there are many major islandwide festivals, celebrating local village festivals remains a strong tradition. Feast days of the local saints provide Cypriots with a good excuse for a party. Most festivals are celebrated with a procession, followed by a feast and much drinking, dancing, and merrymaking. Traditionally this would always have occurred in the village, and many town dwellers would return to their ancestral village to participate in local festivals. However, with increased urbanization, city festivals have become more important.

Opposite: **The Epiphany parade held by the St. Lazarus church in Larnaca.**

Left: **A young girl receives blessings from a priest.**

A priest passes around the flame. It is considered good luck to get home with the candle still alight, to trace a sooty sign of the cross over the threshold of the home.

GREEK ORTHODOX FESTIVALS

Among Greek Cypriots, the Orthodox religion plays a central role in the history, identity, and life of the community. Many age-old pagan festivals have over the centuries been given an Orthodox interpretation, while maintaining notable pagan elements. New Year's Day, for example, is celebrated with the feast of *Ayios Vasílios*, or Saint Basil (A.D. 329–379), one of the spiritual fathers of the Orthodox church feted throughout the Orthodox world. Saint Basil is the Cypriot equivalent of Santa Claus. Gifts are exchanged on this day rather than Christmas.

Epiphany on January 6 marks the baptism of Christ in the River Jordan. It is called *Fóta* ("FOH-tah") by Cypriots, meaning illumination. On this day, holy water fonts in churches are blessed to banish the evil spirits that are said to have lurked on earth since Christmas. The festival is also marked with the baking of doughnuts. It is customary to throw the first doughnut on the roof of the house to scare away any lingering evil spirits. In seaside towns, the celebration reaches a finale when the local bishop throws a crucifix far out into the water and young men swim for the honor of recovering it. March 25 fulfills the dual function of celebrating Greek Independence Day and the feast of the Annunciation.

Easter is the most important celebration in the Greek Orthodox calendar. Many festivals are linked to the Easter festivities. Green Monday, a pre-Lenten carnival, lasts for 10 days in early March. The celebration is held in Limassol and kicks off with the carnival king's entrance to the town on a float, followed by fancy-dress parades, games, and much feasting. After Green Monday, Easter observances begin with Lenten fasting for a full 50 days.

Orthodox Good Friday, which falls a week later than that of the Western Christian churches, is marked by processions through the villages led by a coffin containing a figure of Christ. Village women prepare elaborate floral decorations for the funeral bier. Every icon is draped in black cloth to mark the crucifixion. On Saturday night, huge bonfires are lit, and villagers gather in the local church to celebrate the Resurrection. Everyone holds a candle, while the children hold sparklers. At midnight the priest announces Christ's Resurrection, and eternal life for all believers. The priest passes around a lighted flame, which is handed from worshipper to worshipper. The Lenten fast is broken immediately after the service, with the eating of egg and lemon soup and the cracking of dyed eggs. On Easter Sunday, preparations get underway for the baking of special holiday cakes, *flaoúnes* ("flah-OON-ehs"), a pastry filled with egg, cheese, and raisins.

A family celebrates Orthodox Easter Sunday with a barbecue.

LAND OF MĪRACLES

On Assumption Day, August 15, and St. Andrew's Day, November 30, many pilgrims—both Christians and Muslims—pay a visit to the Apostolos Andreas monastery (monastery of St. Andrew), near the tip of the Karpas Peninsula. The monastery has a reputation as the "Lourdes" of Cyprus, where pilgrims seek cures for their afflictions. The reputation stems from a visit to the spot by the apostle Saint Andrew, the great miracle worker and protector of travelers. He is thought to have stopped here to fetch water while on a trip to preach Christianity in Greece. After restoring the sight of the one-eyed captain of his ship with the water, Andrew is said to have converted and baptized the crew. As a result, a chapel was built in the 15th century at the tiny spring in a nearby rock grotto thought to have healing powers. For many years, it was rumored that the site could heal blindness, deafness, and illnesses of all kinds.

During the Festival of the Flood, people crowd into the sea and sprinkle each other with water, to commemorate the salvation of Noah and the ark from the biblical floods.

The Festival of the Flood, or *Kataklismós* ("kaht-ah-klees-MOHS"), is unique to Cyprus and is celebrated seven weeks after Easter. Elsewhere in the Orthodox world it is merely Pentecost, but in Cyprus it becomes a week-long celebration, especially in coastal towns.

The Assumption of the Virgin, on August 15, marks the rise to heaven of the Virgin Mary and is an important Orthodox festival. The day is celebrated with fairs in many villages and monasteries. Christmas is a far less important holiday in the Orthodox church, and relatively subdued in Cyprus. Western-style commercialization has changed the Christmas celebrations in recent years, and it is now more common to give and receive presents. The most durable traditional custom is the singing of carols—children go door-to-door, singing and accompanied by a triangle.

Other Orthodox festivals are also celebrated—St. Anthony's Day, which honors the Egyptian father of the monastic life, is marked in Nicosia and Limassol on January 17, while St. George's Day on April 23 is celebrated almost everywhere on the island. Apart from islandwide Orthodox festivals, many other celebrations are held locally throughout Cyprus, to honor the local patron saint or holy figure of a monastery. These include the Erection of the Holy Cross at the Stavrovouni monastery on September 14, and the celebration of Saints Peter and Paul in Paphos on June 29, attended by the archbishop and other bishops of the island. St. Neophytos's Day (January 24), which honors the Cypriot religious figure, is feted with a massive procession ending at the famous hermit's cave north of Paphos.

MUSLIM FESTIVALS

In north Cyprus, all major Islamic festivals are celebrated according to the lunar calendar, meaning that the festival recedes by 11 days each year. *Seker Bayrami* ("sheh-kehr bay-rah-MIH"), meaning the sugar festival, because of the great amount of sweets eaten at this time, is celebrated at the end of the fasting month, Ramadan. This three-day holiday is commonly celebrated with a family get-together and the distribution of sweets and presents to the children. *Kurban Bayrami* ("kehr-bahn bay-rah-MIH"), the Feast of the Sacrifice, commemorates Abraham's willingness to sacrifice his son Ishmael, and usually occurs two months after *Seker Bayrami*. Traditionally, families sacrifice a sheep or chicken, which is then eaten at a large family gathering. *Kurban Bayrami* is usually a four-day national holiday, the longest of the year. The Muslim new year and *Mevlûd* ("mehv-LUHD"), or the birth of the Prophet, are also celebrated.

Although Turkish Cypriots celebrate major Muslim festivals, they are not as strict in their observances as some of their neighbors in the Middle East.

Shopping for sweets before the sugar festival.

NONRELIGIOUS FESTIVALS

THE REPUBLIC OF CYPRUS hosts many nonreligious festivals, especially in the summer. While some of these celebrations have a traditional or pagan origin, many of them have been revamped and promoted by the tourist authorities to attract ever increasing numbers of visitors. The most important city festival in Cyprus is the Limassol Wine Festival, held for 12 days every September. The city's municipal gardens become the site for contemporary Dionysiac revelry, where visitors pay an entrance fee that entitles them to sample any of the wines available and attend all the musical and theatrical activities. All the island's wineries are present, offering wine to all who want it. Beer festivals are also organized. During these festivals, beer is sold at a reduced price and consumed along with Cypriot snacks, to the accompaniment of traditional dancing and music.

In May, virtually every town holds a flower festival. The festivities include colorful processions though the streets and competitions for the best flower arrangements. Harvest festivals are also a common feature in some of the larger villages on the island. The whole district will celebrate with singing, feasting, and dancing in the village square. The more tourist-oriented Paphos Festival of Music, Theater, and Dance is staged in the medieval castle and ancient odeon theater of the town from June to September. Limassol also hosts an International Arts Festival in June and July. The Curium Drama Festival takes place in July and August. Overlooking the sea, the 2,000-year-old theater at Curium provides a spectacular setting for the staging of ancient Greek dramas and works by Shakespeare and modern dramatists.

On October 1, Cyprus's Independence Day is celebrated to mark the island's independence, while Greek Independence Day is celebrated on March 25, in solidarity with their brethren on the mainland.

THE TURKISH NORTH In the north, many official holidays have been imported from the Turkish mainland. However, unlike the south, there simply is no budget to hold large and lavish celebrations. Thus most festivals are low-key affairs. Many Turkish Cypriot holidays mark significant events in the Turkish struggle against the Greek desire for *enosis*, such as TMT Day, or the birth of Turkish Cypriot resistance, on August 1, as well as political events such as the 1974 invasion. The festival commemorating the invasion is called Peace and Freedom Day, and falls on July 20. Harvest festivals in the villages on the Mesaoria Plain are probably the most lively events, celebrated to mark the harvesting of the orange, strawberry, and watermelon crops.

Participants in a festive parade in Paphos.

FOOD

FOR CYPRIOTS, FOOD AND DRINK are an essential part of every social occasion, whether a wedding celebration, festival, family gathering, or meeting between friends. Virtually every conversation and meeting is accompanied by coffee, beer or brandy, and snacks.

Cypriot food is generally considered hearty rather than refined, with an emphasis on a wide variety of simple and tasty, home-cooked fare. It reflects a broad range of influences that are the product of Cyprus's history and geographic location. Middle Eastern, Southern European, and British influences can all be detected. Cypriot food draws most strongly on the culinary traditions of Greece and Turkey, from where most of the dishes derive. Lamb and chicken are the most popular meats, and seafood is widely eaten. Grilling and frying are the usual methods of cooking. Olive oil is used generously in Cypriot cuisine, for both cooking and garnishing. Almost all meals are eaten with bread, fried or grilled vegetables, and salad.

Opposite: **Selling jars of homemade honey. Cypriots believe that good traditional Cypriot cuisine is mostly cooked at home.**

Left: **Cypriots having some drinks in a café. The main meal of the day is eaten in the evening, most often late, at around 10 p.m.**

THE GREEK CYPRIOT TABLE

Traditionally, Cypriots ate a simple rural diet of bread, olives, and yogurt, accompanied by cheese, tomatoes and cucumbers. The dish was drizzled with salt, olive oil, and lemon. Today, Cyprus's new-found wealth has resulted in a richer, more varied diet for most Cypriots.

Meat is usually the highlight of any Greek Cypriot meal. Game, including duck, pigeon, quail, and rabbit, is the favorite, but is only eaten on special occasions. *Souvlakia* ("soov-LAH-kee-yah"), or lamb roasted on a spit, often forms the culinary focus of any big gathering. *Kleftikó* ("glehf-tee-KOH"), which is lamb or goat roasted with an assortment of vegetables in an outdoor oven, is probably the nearest thing to a national dish on the island. Every farmhouse and many other houses will have an outdoor oven for the preparation of this dish. Sausages, another popular choice, come in various forms—*sheftalia* ("shehf-TAHL-yah") is grilled sausage made from ground meat, while *pastourmas* ("past-oor-MAHS") is a garlic sausage made from pork. The classic Greek Cypriot meat dish is *souvlaki* ("soov-LAHK-ee"), a kebab made of small cubes of grilled lamb on skewers, often garnished with lemon and salt. Fried meatballs, or *keftedes* ("kehf-TEH-dehs"), complete the typical Cypriot meat selection.

Bread is an essential part of the Cypriot meal and is always first served as a complement to the expected courses. The *pitta* ("PEE-tah")—a flat, crescent-shaped, hollow bread—is most often eaten filled with salad or vegetables and *souvlakia*. Vegetable dishes are usually either grilled or fried in oil, garnished with herbs, and mixed with a little tomato and olive oil. Favorites include stuffed or plain *kolokithakia* ("koh-loh-kee-THA-

Greek salad accompanies most meals and consists of cabbage, lettuce, celery, cucumbers, tomatoes, peppers, olives, *feta* ("FEH-ta") cheese, and herbs, roughly chopped and mixed together, and liberally garnished with olive oil and lemon.

kyah") or squash, *koukia* ("koo-KYAH") or broad beans, and *koupepia* ("koo-PEH-pyah") or vine leaves filled with rice and formed into rolls. *Moussakas* ("moo-sah-KAHS")—layered ground beef, potatoes, and slices of eggplant, baked in a white sauce with a cheese topping—is popular.

Cyprus has a number of puréed dips that can be eaten either with a full meal or as a snack, usually with *pitta* bread. These include *hummos* ("HOO-mohs"), or chickpeas puréed and mixed with garlic and lemon, *taramas* ("tah-rah-MAHS"), a pink, fish roe pâté made with potato purée, lemon, and onions, *talatoúra* ("tah-lah-TOO-rah"), a yogurt, cucumber, and herb dip that is very cooling and especially good with spicy meat dishes, and *tahini* ("tah-HEE-nee"), or sesame seed paste.

While Cypriots are less inclined to eat snacks compared to their mainland Greek and Turkish counterparts, baked tidbits are popular. In the south, these include *kolokótes* ("koh-loh-KOH-tehs"), a triangular pastry stuffed with pumpkin, cracked wheat, and raisins; *takhinopitta* ("tah-chee-NOH-pee-tah"), a pastry with sesame paste; and *eliópitta* ("ehl-YOH-pee-tah"), an olive turnover.

There is no particular order to eating Greek Cypriot cuisine, although sweets are usually eaten last.

MEZE

Cypriots love to share a mixture of as many assorted dishes as possible. This style of dining is known as *meze* ("meh-ZEE"), meaning "mixture." *Meze* is the most popular way of entertaining in the home, and is a feature of every restaurant and tavern menu. *Meze* usually includes a little of everything that is in the kitchen that day. In this way, it provides an excellent introduction to Cypriot cooking. A typical *meze* will usually include fried or grilled fish, *keftedes* and other kinds of kebabs, *sheftalia, pastourmas, hirómeri* ("hee-ROH-meh-ree") or cured local ham, calamari (fried squid rings), *hummos, taramas, tahini*, Greek salad, beans, pickled cauliflower, olives, any number of vegetable dishes, and great quantities of bread. Often, a few Cypriot specialties will be included, in particular *halumi* ("hah-LOO-mih"), a rubbery goat cheese that is often served grilled or just eaten simply with bread and salad. It tastes especially good when fried. The great quantity of food and the vast array of tastes represent a test of appetite and endurance for even the most enthusiastic diner. This, more than any reason, is why Cypriots linger so long over their meals. The whole meal will be washed down with plenty of wine or beer.

TURKISH CUISINE

Turkish Cypriot cuisine owes its heritage to a mixture of Middle Eastern and Southern European influences. While having the same fundamental characteristics as Greek Cypriot food, since partition, the food in the north has become increasingly influenced by mainland tastes. As in the republic, *meze*, including Turkish variations such as *humus, tarama, tahin,* and *cacik* ("jah-CHIK") or *talatoúra*, is extremely popular. Other more typical Turkish dishes include *yalanci dolma* ("yah-lahn-CHI dohl-MAH"), similar to *koupepia*, where vine leaves are stuffed with rice, onions, and tomatoes; *musakka* ("moo-sah-KAH"), similar to the Greek Cypriot dish; and *lazböregi* ("lahz-behr-reh-YEH"), or meat-filled crepes topped with

Like their Greek counterparts, Turkish Cypriots like to eat kebabs with bread.

yogurt. Turkish kebabs come in many varieties, including the ubiquitous *sish kebab* ("sheesh keh-BAHP"), or marinated lamb skewered and grilled over charcoal; and the *köfte* ("kehrf-TEH"), or spiced meatballs. Seafood is also popular. Fresh lobster, crab, mussels, squid, rock bream, and sea bass can be found in the north, though they are expensive.

Salads and vegetable dishes typically include tomatoes, eggplant, red onions, cucumbers, peppers, olives, and radishes. *Fasulye piyaz* ("fahs-uhl-YEH pih-YAHZ"), a haricot bean salad topped with olives and hard-boiled eggs, is a common accompaniment to meals or as part of a *meze*. The curiously named *imam bayaldi* ("ih-MAHM bah-yahl-DIH"), meaning "the imam fainted," is a traditional dish of baked eggplant cut in strips and stuffed with onions, garlic, and tomatoes. Street vendors sell *börek* ("behr-EHK"), a rich, flaky pastry containing bits of meat or cheese. Homemade and sold on the street, *börek* is the pride of Turkish Cypriot cuisine.

Above: **In the north, Turkish delight is a popular snack and dessert, often stuffed with walnuts or pistachios.**

Right: **Homemade almond sweets,** *soudzoúkou.*

SWEETS

Cypriot desserts tend to be extremely sweet and are usually made with local fruit, honey, syrup, and pastry. *Soudzoúkou* ("sood-ZOO-koo"), a confection of almonds strung together and dipped in grape molasses and rosewater, are sold everywhere. *Baklavas* ("pah-klah-VAHS") is the classic Cypriot sweet, made of filo pastry layers alternating with honey and nuts. *Daktila* ("dahk-tee-LAH"), a finger-shaped strudel pastry filled with cinnamon and dipped in syrup, is also common. *Halvas* ("hahl-VAHS") is a sweet made from a grainy paste of semolina or *tahini*, while *loukoumades* ("loo-koo-MAH-dehs") consists of deep-fried balls of choux pastry served in syrup. *Glyká* ("glee-KAH") is a kind of preserved candied fruit, made with either cherries, oranges, or figs, usually only made at village festivals. The Paphos district is famous for *loukoumia* ("loo-koo-MYAH"), or cubes of gelatin served in rosewater and covered with powdered sugar.

FRUIT

Cypriot fruit has a well-deserved reputation for tastiness. Fruit is sold in roadside stalls and in all the town bazaars. The warm climate and long growing season means that Cypriot varieties tend to arrive at the market well before their counterparts in Europe, usually in April. In the south, strawberries are available all year round. Peaches, apricots, watermelon, and desert melons are also grown, as are plums and cherries. The many varieties of cherries grown on the foothills of the Troodos Mountains are delicious. Grapes appear in the early autumn, a by-product of the republic's successful wine industry. Apples, pears, figs, almonds, cherries, lemons, and oranges are also used in Cypriot cooking. Exotic fruit not native to Cyprus, such as avocados, bananas, and kiwis, have been introduced to the warmer corners of the Paphos district. Despite the importance of agriculture to the northern economy, much of the fruit is imported from Turkey, partly because of the inefficiency and backwardness of local farming methods.

DRINKS

A feature of island life since the Ottoman invasion is Turkish coffee—*kafés* ("kah-FEHS") in Greek, *kahve* ("kah-VEH") in Turkish. It is widely drunk on both sides of the partition, though in the south it is generally referred to as Greek or Cypriot coffee, despite its Turkish origins. The fine ground coffee is boiled, then poured straight into a small cup without filtering and drunk either with sugar or neat, leaving a muddy residue at the bottom of the cup. Ideally, it is said that coffee should be drunk as sweet as sin, as hot as hell, and as dark as night. Since the arrival of settlers from Anatolia, the custom of brewing loose-leafed tea is becoming more popular in the villages of the north. Otherwise, tea is not a popular drink. Cyprus also produces its own mineral water—the Troodos and Kyrenia mountains are both famous for their mountain springs, and some water is bottled and sold islandwide. Another popular drink sold by street vendors in Nicosia and Larnaca is *aïráni* ("ah-ee-RAHN-ee"), a refreshing concoction of diluted yogurt mixed with dried mint or oregano.

TALATOÚRA

2 tablespoons olive oil
1 tablespoon vinegar
1 clove garlic, crushed
6 oz (175 g) natural yogurt
2 inch (5 cm) piece of cucumber, finely diced
A pinch of salt
3–4 fresh mint leaves, finely chopped

Lightly beat the oil, vinegar, and garlic with a fork in a bowl. Add the yogurt and beat until smooth and well blended. Add cucumber, a pinch of salt, and chopped mint. Mix well and serve chilled.

Traditionally, Cypriots only drink alcohol as an accompaniment to a meal. Wine is normally drunk with meals in the day, even for breakfast, while on special occasions beer and brandy will be drunk. The wine of the south is of a very high standard, owing to the island's near perfect climate and the long tradition of wine-making. Most of the vineyards are on the slopes of the Troodos Mountains, around Paphos and Limassol. More than 30,000 Cypriot families are involved in grape production, as are a few famous monasteries such as Panagia Chrysorrogiatissa, near Pano Panagia in the western Troodos. More than 40 different wines are produced in the republic, a large number for a small country. Some 30 countries import Cypriot wine, Britain being the largest.

The best varieties of wine include the dry white varieties Arsinoë, Palomino, and White Lady, and the Bellapais medium sparkling wine. Among red wines, Othello and Rosella are common table wines. Commandaria is the most famous wine on the island. It is produced using the age-old method of fermentation in open jars. The same jars are repeatedly used, so that each new batch contains a trace of traditional quality.

It is said that in 1570, the Turkish Sultan, Selim, was so intoxicated by his desire for the wine that he launched the Ottoman invasion on the island. Sherries are also produced, the most famous being the Emva brand. Local wine is also made in microwineries in the villages and monasteries of the Troodos, and drunk from the barrel.

Talatoúra *is an extremely refreshing and fragrant dish ideally eaten with either kebabs, fried slices of eggplant or squash, or just as a dip with bread. It is a standard feature of the Cypriot meze.*

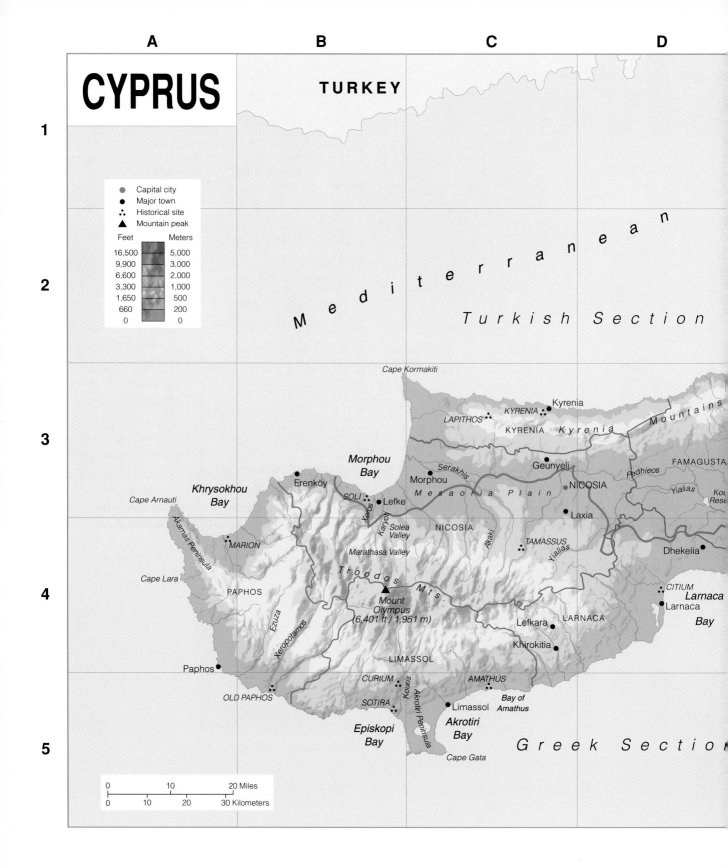

CYPRUS

TURKEY

Capital city
Major town
Historical site
Mountain peak

Feet	Meters
16,500	5,000
9,900	3,000
6,600	2,000
3,300	1,000
1,650	500
660	200
0	0

Mediterranean

Turkish Section

Cape Kormakiti

KYRENIA · Kyrenia

LAPITHOS

KYRENIA *Kyrenia Mountains*

Morphou Bay

Serakhis

Morphou

Geunyeli

Mesaoria Plain • NICOSIA

FAMAGUSTA

Pedhieos

Khrysokhou Bay

Erenköy

• Erenköy

SOLI · Lefke

Xeros

Yialias

Kou Rese

Cape Arnauti

Akamas Peninsula

Kanyon

Solea Valley

NICOSIA

• Laxia

Cape Lara

MARION

Marathasa Valley

Akaki

TAMASSUS

Yialias

Dhekelia

PAPHOS

Ezuza

Troodos

Mts.

▲ Mount Olympus
(6,401 ft / 1,951 m)

CITIUM

Larnaca

Xeropotamos

LARNACA

Larnaca Bay

Lefkara •

Paphos •

LIMASSOL

Khirokitia •

CURIUM

Kouris

AMATHUS

OLD PAPHOS

SOTIRA

Akrotiri Peninsula

Kryos

• Limassol

Bay of Amathus

Episkopi Bay

Akrotiri Bay

Greek Section

Cape Gata

0	10	20 Miles
0	10	20	30 Kilometers

E F

Cape Andreas

Cape Plakoti

Karpas Peninsula

Cape Elea

Famagusta

LAMIS *Bay*

Famagusta
•Varosha

•Paralimni

Ayia Napa

Cape Greco

N

Akaki River, C4
Akamas Peninsula, A4
Akrotiri Bay, C5
Akrotiri Peninsula, C5
Amathus, Bay of, C5
Amathus Historical Site, C5
Andreas, Cape, F2
Arnauti, Cape, A3
Ayia Napa, E4

Citium Historical Site, D4
Curium Historical Site, B5

Dhekelia, D4

Elea, Cape, E3
Episkopi Bay, B5
Erenköy, B3
Ezuza River, B4

Famagusta, E3
Famagusta Bay, E3
Famagusta District, D3

Gata, Cape, C5
Geunyeli, C3
Greco, Cape, E4

Karpas Peninsula, E2–F2
Karyoti River, B3–B4
Khirokitia, C4
Khrysokhou Bay, A3
Kormakiti, Cape, B3–C3
Kouklia Reservoir, D3
Kouris River, B5
Kyrenia, C3
Kyrenia District, C3
Kyrenia Historical Site, C3
Kyrenia Mountains, C3–D3

Lapithos Historical Site, C3
Lara, Cape, A4
Larnaca, D4

Larnaca Bay, D4
Larnaca District, C4–D4
Laxia, C3
Lefkara, C4
Lefke, B3
Limassol, C5
Limassol District, B4–C4

Marathasa Valley, B4
Marion Historical Site, A4
Mediterranean Sea, B2–E1
Mesaoria Plain, C3
Morphou, C3
Morphou Bay, B3

Nicosia, C3
Nicosia District, C4

Old Paphos Historical
  Site, B5
Olympus, Mount, B4

Paphos, A4
Paphos District, A4–B4
Paralimni, E4
Pedhieos River, D3
Plakoti, Cape, E2

Salamis Historical Site, E3
Serakhis River, C3
Solea Valley, B4
Soli Historical Site, B3
Sotira Historical Site, B5

Tamassus Historical Site, C4
Troodos Mountains, B4–C4
Turkey, B1

Varosha, E3

Xeropotamos River, B4
Xeros River, B3

Yialias River, C4–D3

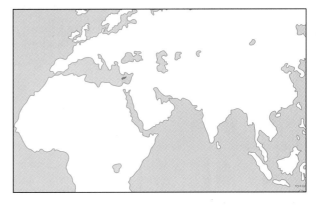

QUICK NOTES

OFFICIAL NAMES
Republic of Cyprus (*Kypriaki Dimokratia*)
Turkish Republic of North Cyprus (*Kuzey Kibris Türk Cumhuriyeti*—not recognized by the United Nations)

TOTAL LAND AREA
3,572 square miles (9,251 square km)

TOTAL POPULATION
775,000 people (1997 estimate)

POPULATION GROWTH RATE
1.08% (1997 estimate)

CAPITAL
Nicosia

MAJOR CITIES
Limassol, Larnaca, Paphos, Famagusta, Kyrenia

DISTRICTS
Nicosia, Limassol, Larnaca, Paphos, Famagusta, Kyrenia

HISTORICAL SITES
Amathus, Citium, Curium, Kyrenia, Lapithos, Marion, Old Paphos, Salamis, Soli, Sotira, Tamassus

MOUNTAIN RANGES
Troodos, Kyrenia

RIVERS
Pedhieos, Yialias, Karyoti, Kouris

CLIMATE
Mediterranean

HIGHEST POINT
Mount Olympus (6,401 ft / 1,951 m)

MAIN RELIGIONS
Greek Orthodox, Islam

LANGUAGES
Republic of Cyprus—official language Greek; English widely spoken.
TRNC—official language Turkish; Greek and English also spoken.

CURRENCY
Republic of Cyprus—Cyprus pound (CY£)
US$1 = CY£0.5386 (1999)
TRNC—Turkish lira (TL)
US$1 = TL379,820 (1999)

MAIN EXPORTS
Republic of Cyprus—citrus fruit, grapes, wine, potatoes, cement, clothing, shoes
TRNC—citrus fruit, potatoes, textiles

MAIN IMPORTS
Republic of Cyprus—food, petroleum, machinery
TRNC—food, minerals, chemicals, machinery

POLITICAL LEADERS
President of the Republic of Cyprus—Glafkos Clerides
President of the TRNC—Rauf Denktash

GLOSSARY

baklavas ("pah-klah-VAHS")
A popular Cypriot sweet made of filo pastry layers alternating with honey and nuts.

cepken ("chep-KEHN")
Short, embroidered vests worn by Turkish Cypriot men.

enosis ("EH-noh-sees")
A Greek word meaning "unification."

Fóta ("FOH-tah")
The Greek name for the Orthodox celebration of Epiphany in January.

hummos ("HOO-mohs")
A popular dip consisting of chickpeas puréed and mixed with garlic and lemon.

kapheneia ("gahf-EHN-ee-ah") / **kahve** ("kah-VEH")
The Greek and Turkish names respectively for the ubiquitous coffeehouses found on every street corner.

karpasitiko ("karp-ahs-IHT-ih-koh")
Popular traditional dress worn by Greek Cypriot women.

kartchilamas ("gar-chee-LAH-mahs")
A popular Cypriot dance performed by facing pairs of male and female dancers.

Kataklismós ("kaht-ah-klees-MOHS")
The Festival of the Flood, celebrated in the Orthodox Church seven weeks after Easter.

Kurban Bayrami ("kehr-bahn bay-rah-MIH")
Muslim feast of the Sacrifice.

meze ("meh-ZEE")
A style of dining, where a little of everything cooked that day is eaten as a shared meal.

misafir ("mihs-ah-FEER")
Turkish word for "guest."

pitharia ("PIH-thah-ree-ah")
Large, traditional Cypriot earthenware containers used for storing olives, wine, and olive oil.

pitta ("PEE-tah")
A flat, hollow bread, most often eaten filled with salad or vegetables and *souvlakia*.

Seker Bayrami ("sheh-kehr bay-rah-MIH")
The Muslim feast celebrating the end of the fasting month of Ramadan. *Seker Bayrami* means "sugar festival."

shalvar ("shahl-VAHR")
Baggy trousers worn by Turkish Cypriot men and women.

souvlakia ("soov-LAH-kee-yah")
Lamb roasted on a spit.

soudzoúkou ("sood-ZOO-koo")
Almonds strung together and dipped in grape molasses and rosewater.

taksim ("tahk-SIHM")
A Turkish word meaning "partition."

BIBLIOGRAPHY

Brey H. and Müller C. (editors). *Insight Guides: Cyprus*. Hongkong: APA Publications, 1995.

Darke, Diana. *Guide to North Cyprus*. Chalfont St. Peter, UK: Bradt Publications, 1993.

Durrell, Lawrence. *Bitter Lemons*. New York: Penguin Books, 1991.

McDonald, George. *Cyprus*. London: AA Essential Explorer series, AA Publishing, 1995.

Thubron, Colin. *Journey into Cyprus*. Harmondsworth: Penguin Books, 1986.

INDEX

INDEX

INDEX

PICTURE CREDITS
Archive Photos: 24 (top), 26, 32, 33, 34, 35, 36, 37, 50, 71, 73, 88
Camera Press: 30, 31
Christine Osborne Pictures: 39
Focus Team, Italy: 5, 7, 12 (bottom), 49, 55, 62, 63, 67, 80, 84, 96, 97, 105, 106, 114, 120
Dave G. Houser: 24 (bottom), 53, 68, 89, 90, 95, 112
Hutchison Library: 4, 66, 76, 77
North Wind Picture Archives: 22
Photobank: 6, 8, 11, 14, 18, 19, 20, 40, 69, 70, 75, 85, 86, 87, 93, 94, 100, 113, 119
David Simson: 10, 48, 99, 117
Topham Picturepoint: 16, 38, 41, 42, 44, 46, 57, 60, 64, 92, 109
Trip Photographic Agency: 1, 3, 12 (top), 21, 23, 27, 28, 43, 45, 47, 51, 52, 54, 58, 59, 74, 78, 82, 83, 98, 103, 104, 107, 110, 111, 115, 116, 118 (both)